Utopia and Modernity in China

'For a China mired in the past, even by language, to imagine a utopia of a modern future took major reinventions of thought, expression and outlook. This extremely difficult process, unappreciated in the West but probably unparalleled in modern history, is superbly charted in this important collection.'

—Stephen Chan OBE, Professor of World Politics, SOAS University of London

'The debate about China's destination has been raging for nearly 200 years. This book makes a valuable contribution to our understanding of the diverse possibilities in the evolution of China's identity.'

—Professor Hugo de Burgh, Walt Disney Chair in Global Media and Communications, Tsinghua University

'The current Cold War climate that sees China as a threat, and little else, makes it all the more important to understand China on its own terms. The book avoids simplistic accounts and presents important insights into Chinese visions of itself.'

—Anthony Welch, Professor of Education, University of Sydney

Utopia and Modernity in China

Contradictions in Transition

Edited by
David Margolies and Qing Cao

First published 2022 by Pluto Press
New Wing, Somerset House, Strand, London WC2R 1LA

www.plutobooks.com

British Library Cataloguing in Publication Data
A catalogue record for this book is available from the British Library

ISBN 978 0 7453 4158 3 Hardback
ISBN 978 0 7453 4739 4 Paperback
ISBN 978 1 786808 34 9 PDF
ISBN 978 1 786808 35 6 EPUB eBook

This book is printed on paper suitable for recycling and made from fully managed and sustained forest sources. Logging, pulping and manufacturing processes are expected to conform to the environmental standards of the country of origin.

Typeset by Stanford DTP Services, Northampton, England

Simultaneously printed in the United Kingdom and United States of America

Contents

Preface

There are many difficulties in managing a project conducted across two countries with two very different languages and cultures, even in a world supposedly united by electronic communication. The people for whom this has been most obvious are the co-editor of the book, Dr Qing Cao, and Dr Min Zhao, our coordinator in China, who had to negotiate across the two cultures and languages. Without Dr Cao's cross-cultural knowledge and his wise judgement the project would simply not have been possible. Without Dr Zhao's understanding, persistence and sympathy, it would never have progressed beyond the 'good idea' stage.

A debt of gratitude is also owed to our translator, Charles Collins, whose long experience of both English and Chinese cultures has made him familiar with popular as well as standard, polite usage and who willingly spent hours discussing how Chinese concepts and expressions could best be rendered in English.

Finally, our authors must be thanked for their patience and for their commitment to the principle that their work should contribute to a better world.

David Margolies
June 2021

Introduction

David Margolies and Qing Cao

China today is more important to the world than ever before, and in the last decade Western interest in and media attention on China have been growing at an ever-increasing pace.* China's economic power has long been recognised, as has its technological innovation and ability to complete massive construction projects with unmatchable speed. Its global reach has become so extended as to make the West uneasy – from infrastructure loans to African and South American countries to an Antarctic base and a bid on renovating Greenland's airfields. The US is engaging in what is being called a new Cold War against China, joined (though half-heartedly) by the UK, and in both countries human rights issues have been raised to unprecedented prominence. China's management of the Covid-19 crisis has been the most successful of the larger countries, whereas governments in both the US and UK have patently failed to deal with it adequately. Their admiration for China's success in this respect, however, is tempered by prejudices regarding state control of people's lives: China's success in controlling the pandemic is often popularly attributed to repressive control, or its people's fear of it.

This interest in China is not matched by understanding. At professional levels the West may know a great deal about China but among the general population it seems that tabloid- and television-driven prejudices rule. China is the world's oldest continuous civilisation. That continuity suggests overtones of peace and tranquility, but its last century was anything but tranquil – it was a century of revolution. The Xinhai Revolution of 1911 established a republic and put an end to dynastic structures. After the defeat of the Japanese in the

* The research in this book was supported by a grant of the National Social Science Fund of China, and the 'Open World Research Initiative' grant of the Arts and Humanities Research Council in the UK.

Second World War, Chairman Mao Zedong led the Communist Party of China in the War of Liberation which resulted in the proclamation of the People's Republic of China in 1949. Less than two decades later, in 1966, Mao launched the Great Proletarian Cultural Revolution which produced a decade of economic and social turmoil. In 1978 Deng Xiaoping became leader and began a programme of economic modernisation which opened the country to neo-liberalism under the watchful eye of the socialist state. It is important to have some understanding of these transformations, not simply because China is a great power, but because all of us now live in the throes of equivalent transformations: fundamental conflicts of values, economic systems that are failing the general population, and social organisation that is based on inequality. Understanding something of the conflicts involved in China's process of modernisation should be instructive in our own situation. *Utopia and Modernity in China* was conceived in the hope that discussions of those value contradictions embodied in the Chinese experience can provide English-language readers with a perspective useful for making sense of their own condition.

In less than a year, three crises have entered public consciousness in the West. The most obvious, of course, is the Covid-19 pandemic. Because it threatened lives among most of the population, its importance penetrated the barrier of indifference and raised fundamental questions of priorities with regard to the well-being of the population and the economic life of the country. It also raised related questions about government responsibility in matters of health, care for the elderly, children and their education, patterns of work and employment, housing conditions, and the relation between health and the environment. Then, the police murder of George Floyd sparked the rise of the Black Lives Matter movement. That raised another series of questions, some of them related to issues raised by the pandemic – issues people felt that they could do something about. The massive response led to explicit recognition among public and private institutions that structural discrimination was indeed a crisis.

The climate and environment are the third crisis. Despite many writers who, since Rachel Carson's 1962 book *Silent Spring*, have raised their voices about the destruction of the environment and the severe consequences for human life, these issues have been slow to enter public consciousness. Greta Thunberg's high profile and the XR (Extinction Rebellion) protests, which blocked central London traffic, helped raise awareness, and the wildfires and floods of 2021 have shown the crisis to be real and to be global. However, we have yet to see any serious change in practice from governments. But the new willingness of people to question received positions and even to consider different ways of organising society is a very important change.

The questions about social values and social organisation raised by such national and international disruptions are fundamental. They have always been fundamental, but the current crises have brought into consideration across the whole society issues that a few months earlier would have been considered abstract idealism. Perhaps there are alternatives to letting our lives be dominated by the internal combustion engine and personal vehicular transport; perhaps commuting to work should not be a necessary imposition for earning a living. Should everyone have to be an earner to enjoy the benefits of society? What value are we willing to give to clear skies and the return of birdsong? Lockdown has changed our awareness of the centrality of human relationships. The self-justifications of the UK government over its failure to deal effectively with Covid-19 have thrown into question social priorities – not just health vs economy but the fundamental principles on which society should be organised. China's successful management of lockdown was not just a matter of enforcement: China, now as well as traditionally, has a more developed social consciousness – individuals willingly endure their own discomfort when it is necessary for the well-being of the wider population – whereas the UK and US have seen widespread selfish unwillingness to wear masks and observe social distancing.

The opposition of utopia and modernity may appear to have limited significance in the UK and the US, where 'utopia' is usually applied to ideal, unrealisable conditions and 'modernity' primarily refers to being up-to-date (the opposite of 'old fashioned'), the expected condition in modern society. Change and development are the mode of existence; novelty is a major aspect of a consumer society. With regard to China the opposition is more complex. This is partly because modernity was not so much a welcoming of progress as a necessary condition for defending the integrity of the state. The Opium Wars of the nineteenth century had shown that millennia of culture were no defence against the latest military technology, and the definitive defeat of China by Japan in the First Sino-Japanese War (1894–1895) was both a shock and a humiliation. At that point, modernisation was clearly necessary and it could not simply be an 'add-on'. The 'renovation' had to include social culture – the current culture included the ancient, which placed a high value on continuity and shunned confrontation. Thus, the process of modernisation necessarily involved value conflicts at the deepest level.

The West, the obvious model of modernity, was influenced by the Platonic model of social order (but without Plato's caution against self-interest) – a class of rulers was supported by a military class who controlled the general populace. China adopted the Confucian view of social hierarchy: at the top, scholars, then farmers, artisans, and merchants. Force was not an aspect of that order; and, as much as practice may diverge from theory, harmony remains fundamental to the Chinese value system. This is the reverse of the West's view: for China, utopia (in the aspect of harmony) is the expectation, the desired normal, while modernity is the disrupter. This may help to explain the relevance of 'nostalgic utopia' which occurs in several of the chapters in this volume – a longing for a previous world of integration and harmony.

Discussion of utopia and modernity provides a broad framework for evaluating change because it brings together the perspectives of both social values and practicability. It also takes the discussion beyond the disciplinary confines of academia, which have become depressingly narrow. Higher education structures and the criteria for promotion have encouraged individual self-advancement rather than collective endeavour; one of the consequences of this is the growth of specializations so particular that potential audiences, even in what may be nominally the same discipline, are in effect excluded from the discussion.

The surge of awareness of the importance of gender and race and the recognition of the way they have become part of institutional structures has been accompanied by a rather slower growth of understanding of how gender and race become part of the emotional structure of individuals, locked into the language they use and shaping their thinking. The authors of the following chapters take their arguments beyond the conventional limits of their academic disciplines. We hope their perspectives will be helpful in making sense of the perilous state of our world.

MODERNITY AS RUPTURE

China's cultural traditions developed over two thousand years, providing people with a coherent view of the world and their proper place in it. Confucianism provided a model of interpersonal relations with an emphasis on harmony; Taoism advanced respect for nature, or the cosmic 'Way', as a guide for human survival; and Buddhism stressed that the regulation of human desires was a condition of the fulfilled life. However, these perspectives were displaced by the revolutions of the twentieth century. From the 1911 Xinhai Revolution through the 1919 May Fourth Movement, and on to the 1949 Communist Revolution, they gradually lost their central position. A spiritual vacuum and a crisis of identity were produced, a counterpart of China's single-minded drive to industrialise and to achieve a national revival.

The search for values to fill the void allowed China to become a vast arena of experimentation with Western ideas and ideologies – social Darwinism, scientism and anarchism, liberalism and democracy, as well as socialism and communism. All found advocates, but socialism proved the most durable and became the official ideology of the post-1949 People's Republic of China. However, this was not without conflict. As the Tsinghua University cultural critic Gan Yang summarises the situation,[1] there exist three key strands of the value system in contemporary China: Maoist egalitarianism (orthodox socialism), post-reform market-based liberalism under the socialist state ('socialism with Chinese characteristics'), and values based on traditional culture. Despite efforts by many to reconcile them, the competing systems remain and have produced the hybrid value system that guides the current policies.

The transformation from the traditional '*tianxia*' ('all under heaven') universalist state to a modern nation-state has entailed a fundamental shift from a cultural to a political China, where the bond between people is defined less by shared cultural heritage than by identification with the political community of a modern republic. What it means to be Chinese is changing. As the philosopher Tu Weiming notes, 'the China that evokes historical consciousness, cultural continuity, and social harmony, not to mention centredness and rootedness, already seems a distant echo'.[2] The recent resurgence of Confucianism, with its humane values, does not fit easily with the values and lifestyles of modern China; but there are an increasing number of political scientists who believe that China's traditional values may yet lead to a 'contested modernity'[3] or 'multiple modernities'.[4] The Chinese do not accept the Hobbesian view that the state is a necessary evil. Rather, Confucian views are still current, in which the state is viewed as the extension of family and its legitimacy is seen as dependent on the state's moral authority. It is this conflict of values posed by China's transition to a modern state that the chapters of this book explore in diverse manifestations.

THE ORGANISATION OF THE BOOK

Providing a historical context, Chapter 1, Qing Cao's 'The Lure of Utopia: Reinterpreting Liang Qichao's *Xinmin Shuo*, 1902–1906', explains the social and political context of early-twentieth-century China. It discusses the shift of utopian ideals from China's own classical age to the modern West. The material is political and social, the argument focused through the figure of Liang Qichao, an exceptionally influential intellectual in the early decades of the twentieth century. Cao underlines that China's 1895 defeat in the First Sino-Japanese War had been not only a military disaster and a national humiliation; it had also exposed the clash between two knowledge systems and worldviews. What national reform should involve became a matter of intense dispute. The charismatic Liang was a major participant – his newspaper, *Xinmin Congbao*, provided a political platform and he had a large following. The obvious model for reform was the West; but whereas to many people this simply meant adopting Western technology, Liang and his followers believed that the key to successful reform was changing the character and outlook of the Chinese people. Most of the Chinese population were peasants and traditionally saw the world through the perspective of their clan and their local connections, a viewpoint that Liang saw was cripplingly narrow. Cao shows Liang arguing for a wider, Western-type perspective, in which individuals saw themselves as part of a 'national' community, not just of an extended family. It was not just the 'can-do' attitude of the West but also a mentality wherein people saw themselves as citizens and had a national consciousness. Liang had a huge appeal among the literate population of China, even the young Mao Zedong was sufficiently impressed to form his own society of Liang's 'new people'. Cao argues that Liang, despite his current reputation as conservative, contributed inadvertently to intellectual radicalism that has had a deep impact on modern China.

In Chapter 2, 'Utopian Future in Chinese Poetry: Bian Zhilin in Republican China', Yang Zhou focuses on the much-admired poet Bian Zhilin, presenting a more personal and emotional picture of the changing circumstances of the early twentieth century. Bian was active a generation after Liang (their lives overlapped for little more than a decade) but many of the same issues were still present, even if their forms may have changed. Corruption was still very much a problem and the representative democracy of the West still seemed attractive; the imperialist West, however, had inflicted much pain on China and was also an object of hatred. Whereas Liang, as a politician, focused on the masses, Bian, as a poet, was concerned with feelings and an individual response. He was attracted to Western culture, the French symbolist poets in particular. It was the symbolists' precision of imagery and language that he so admired, characteristics that were associated with the traditional Chinese aesthetic. Zhou explains, through closely examining some of Bian's work, how the attractions of modernity and utopia were in conflict. The negative political reality that angered and depressed Bian is illustrated at the level of personal feeling and it is countered in part by nostalgia, a backward-looking glance at traditional Chinese art. Zhou reveals the agony of the Chinese intellectuals torn between a longing for modern changes and a nostalgic return to their spiritual homeland of a classical past.

The third chapter moves into contemporary issues. Yonit Manor-Percival, in 'The China Dream: Harmonious Dialectics and International Law', analyses the imbalance of power and justice that has shaped international law and the contradictions that China has not managed to resolve in becoming a world power. There are fundamental contradictions between the utopian vision introduced by Xi Jinping in his 'China Dream' speech in 2012 and China's participation in international law. Manor-Percival demystifies international law and the popular assumptions that it is neutral (like logic) and an impartial, rational construction. Situating China's international position in its historical quest for modernity, Manor-Percival argues that with international law's roots in colonial encounter and its claims to civilisational universalism it may come into conflict with the Chinese non-prescriptive diversity that derives from China's ancient philosophy.

The contradictions that arise in regard to China's role in international law are not theoretical, they are material, and as such they should provide a context that helps make clear the contradictions of values and attitudes that are displayed in the imaginative works discussed in chapters 4, 5, and 6.

In Chapter 4, 'Nostalgic Utopia in Chinese Aesthetic Modernity: The Case of the Film *Fang Hua* (Youth)', Jie Wang discusses Feng Xiaogang's important 2017 film. The story is taken from a novel by Yan Geling, a Chinese American novelist. It concerns the experience of two people in a military arts troupe (they are part of the military – soldiers – but they are a dance and opera company). The male dancer is a heroic communist whose intense commitment and limited awareness of other people's feelings somewhat alienate him from the rest of the troupe; the female dancer has outstanding talent but is marginalised by the other women, who come from more affluent backgrounds. The dismissive class attitudes toward the protagonists, little more than unpleasant at the time, are developed into a part of the social critique later in the film. Both the protagonists are shown to have behaved with outstanding heroism in the Sino-Vietnamese War (February–March 1979), but on their return to post-war society they find only callous indifference and vicious self-interest in what has become a consumer society.

The context of song and dance allows the director to make exceptional use of music to express the attitudes attached to different periods. Wang describes how this technique functions and explains the associated aesthetic style of 'nostalgic utopia' – the yearning for the idyllic rural life of the past. This was a trope of classical Chinese culture and became a dominant aesthetic in the 1919 May Fourth Movement, continuing in contemporary Chinese films and art. This aesthetic approach facilitates Wang's argument that modernisation has driven out not only traditional but also socialist values.

In Chapter 5, 'American Dreams in China: The Case of *Zhongguo Hehuoren*', Qinghong Yin deals with a 2013 Chinese film that explores how three young men, friends from university, pursue ambitions that bring them into conflict with traditional values. The Chinese title of the film translates as 'The Chinese Partners', but the English title, *American Dreams in China*, is more suggestive of the area of conflict. The film was exceptionally popular but provoked controversy among critics and viewers over its values. Some people welcomed the narrative of a 'loser' making good, especially a Chinese success at the expense of the Americans, but others saw the film as a critique of the individualistic pursuit of financial success, demonstrating a conflict between personal and commercial values. Yin argues the film can be read as the 'national fable' of modern China's gradual rise to prosperity, rather than the story of the success of countless small businesses.

Chapter 6, Jiaona Xu's 'Between Reality and Utopia: Chinese Underclass Literature since the 1990s', examines how several novels treat the motives that drive people from the villages to the cities and how they depict the reality that the migrants encounter. Migration became a massive problem in the period of economic liberation, a very material manifestation of the contradictions between real life and social values. Xu writes about conflicts that are not a matter of value choices; migration comes about because of lack of opportunity – not the kind of opportunity in *American Dreams in China* – but simply the opportunity to make a decent life and escape from the narrow existence of the village. Migration seems the only way out, but migrants are marginalised in the city, without the simple opportunities they imagined, with terrible employment that is insecure, often dangerous, and inadequately remunerated. They have no validity in the social structure. Xu deals with authors who present vividly, at the level of individual experience, the problems faced by the migrants. Xu raises the question of the society's responsibility and suggests that the authors, able to movingly depict the problems of migrants in their novels, have a responsibility also to act on their understanding.

The final chapter, Xiangzhan Cheng's 'Eco-humanism and the Construction of Eco-aesthetics in China', looks at the development of environmental understanding in China. Most of the world recognises that there are dangerous consequences of treating the world around us as simply a source of material to use as we please, but there is still a practice and habit of mind that judges everything in nature in terms of its immediate benefit to humans – nature as a material utopia, a wealth of resources. Traditional Marxism has been guilty of this, emphasising the increase of production without regard to the environment or to Marx's own views against the exploitation of nature as well as humans. Cheng takes what is very much a Chinese perspective on this matter, drawing on ancient Chinese wisdom and a Confucian view of the proper relation of humans to nature. He has put forward the concept of the '*sheng sheng* aesthetic'. *Sheng sheng*, which literally means 'birth and rebirth', has associations which suggest not only sustainability but also inclusiveness – 'all under heaven'. It rejects anthropocentrism – seeing everything in relation to humans – and insists on also understanding things in terms of themselves, and humanity is welcomed as part of this greater harmony. Eco-humanism, more than a passive philosophy, has a practical potential in preserving the life of the planet.

NOTES

1. Gan Yang, *Tong Santong* [Integrating three traditions] (Beijing: Sanlian shudian, 2007).
2. Tu Weiming, preface to *The Living Tree: The Changing Meaning of Being Chinese Today*, ed. Tu Weiming (Stanford: Stanford University Press, 1994), vii.
3. Martin Jaques, *When China Rules the World: The End of the Western World and the Birth of a New Global Order*, 2nd ed. (New York: Penguin, 2012).
4. Kishore Mahbubani, *The Great Convergence: Asia, the West, and the Logic of One World* (New York: Public Affairs, 2013).

1
The Lure of Utopia: Reinterpreting Liang Qichao's *Xinmin Shuo*, 1902–1906

Qing Cao

Liang Qichao (1873–1927) was a central actor in the wave of radicalism that swept China in the first decades of the twentieth century.* In this period, when China changed from an imperial dynasty to a modern republic, he was arguably the most influential cultural leader. As a scholar, journalist, and newspaper editor, and a political reformer and polemist, Liang articulated the feelings of many of the educated class and helped shape the intellectual foundations of modern China. However, Liang remains a controversial figure. Although his advocacy of Western values is seen as positive, in China he was also regarded as a reactionary for his support for a constitutional monarchy and fierce opposition to political revolution.

In most previous studies,[1] Liang's contributions are assessed according to a normative paradigm of 'progress', which assumes an inevitable human path towards modernity, a destined end irrespective of cultural diversities. This chapter moves away from this dominant perspective. Instead, I examine the way in which Liang's writings were subversive, undermining traditional Chinese social attitudes with a utopian view of the West and a negative vision of late Qing society. I argue that Liang's intellectual radicalism stems from a romanticised view of the West and I will use his influential text *Xinmin Shuo* 新民说 (On New People, 1902–1906) as a case study. *Xinmin Shuo* is a series of twenty articles published in Liang's own newspaper *Xinmin Congbao* 新民丛报 (New People Newspaper). Written a few years before the 1911 Xinhai Revolution – a military

* The UK Arts and Humanities Research Council's (AHRC) Open World Research Initiative (OWRI) supported the research and production of this study.

uprising that brought the 2,132-year Chinese empire to an end – these articles detailed a roadmap to transforming traditional China into a Western-style nation-state. As a discourse on the creation of a 'new people' out of China's traditional peasantry, *Xinmin Shuo* became deeply destabilising to China's established cultural order in its fundamental negation of Chinese sociocultural norms. It produced a masterplan to 'save China' by trying to alter the way people thought and behaved through an intellectual campaign of social engineering. Ultimately, the campaign aimed at instilling the alien sense of 'nation' into the popular consciousness, because Liang believed the transformation into a modern nation-state was the only way to free China from its dire predicament.

The year 1895 is a watershed moment in China's modern history. The signing of Shimonoseki Treaty on 23 March 1895 as a settlement of the First Sino-Japanese War (1894–1895) shook China to the core. The victory of Japan, traditionally seen as a cultural disciple of China for over a millennium, symbolised to many elites that there were fundamental flaws in Chinese culture, and it was inadequate in meeting modern challenges. Whilst the Sino-British Opium War of 1839–1842 was treated largely as a nuisance caused by far-flung barbarians, the 1895 debacle triggered a psychological earthquake. The literati class became concerned not with the loss of Taiwan and the Liaodong peninsula, nor the two-hundred-million-silver-tael war indemnity, nor the opening of trading ports of Shashi, Chongqing, Suzhou, and Hangzhou, but with the demise of Chinese order (*wang tianxia* 亡天下). They came to see the Western challenge as a cultural and political issue, rather than a military and technical issue. It was at this point that the political and intellectual elites recognised the failure of the Self-Strengthening Movement (1861–1895) that aimed at adopting Western technology, especially military technology, to build a modern navy and national defence.

The Self-Strengthening Movement was premised on the superiority of a Chinese civilisation that only needed to adopt modern technology. The 1895 defeat demolished the premise. Against this backdrop, a new generation of intellectuals came of age, demanding radical political reforms. Taking centre stage were the young Liang Qichao and his mentor Kang Youwei (1858–1927), who organised public petitions by hundreds of scholars to the Guangxu emperor (1871–1908). For the first time in Chinese history, scholars were intervening in court politics, not through high offices within the system, but through direct appeal to the emperor as members of the public. In late 1898, at the age of twenty-five, Liang became an advisor to the emperor during the brief Hundred Days' Reform that made swift and sweeping changes in the modernisation of the government and its institutions. The disastrous failure of the Hundred Days' Reform, due to a coup by Cixi the Dowager (1835–1908), aborted the political reform. But it spawned an intellectual campaign that shifted the focus to the remaking of society in the image of Europe. It aimed at engineering a 'new people' with strong collective characters capable of organising themselves into a modern nation-state.

Exiled to Japan immediately after his botched political career in late 1898, Liang became the leading light of this intellectual campaign through the newly emergent press. Launching an unapologetic crusade against China's longstanding traditions and popularising Western learning, Liang inaugurated a bottom-up approach to creating a modern nation-state. With the help of his powerful pen and refreshing polemical style, Liang galvanised public opinion in the depths of China's crisis. Exploiting the modern press to the full, he launched his own newspapers, first *Qingyi Bao* 清议报 (1898–1901) and then *Xinmin Congbao* (1902–1907). In pre-1911 China, it was primarily the press that made knowledge about Western social and political ideas available to the public. They captured the intense interest of the young, aspirant educated class. Thanks to Liang and other similarly minded intellectuals, the trickle of Western learning since the 1839–1842 Opium War turned into a torrent that inundated the post-1898 intellectual scene as people intensified their search for a solution to China's crisis. Liang became a crucial agent behind the tidal wave of radicalism that swept across early-twentieth-century China.

LIANG'S INTELLECTUAL CAMPAIGN AND THE DOUBLE SHIFT OF UTOPIA

At the root of Liang's radical campaign lay a fundamental shift in epistemology. This was reflected in part in a double reversal of utopia, in terms of time and location. That is, there was a temporal swing – people no longer sought the sociopolitical ideal in the past but in an envisaged future. There was also a spatial shift from a Chinese source to the West. The word 'utopia' in this chapter is used in both Thomas More's and Karl Mannheim's sense of the term.[2] It refers to an ideal society as in More's *Utopia*, as well as a state of mind that is incongruent with the state of reality. For the first time in China's history, the utopian imagining of social ideals was projected outside China to an outlying Europe – a novel land of hopes, dreams, and aspirations. Unlike the European utopia located in a spatial 'nowhere', traditional China maintained a cardinal boundary between a superior *huaxia* 华夏 (China) and inferior *manyi* 蛮夷 (barbarians). Utopia, if it ever existed, would be found in China, the centre of the known world. Traditionally, in China's three-millennia history, when sociopolitical conditions had badly deteriorated, the scholar-gentry class would look back to the golden age of the *sandai* 三代 (the three dynasties) for guidance and inspiration. The term *sandai* refers to ancient Chinese history before China's unification in 221 BCE. It includes the three dynasties of Xia 夏(2100–1600 BCE), Shang 商(1600–1066 BCE), and Zhou 周(1066–221 BCE). These dynasties became known collectively as the *sandai* – a revered term symbolising the perfect sociopolitical order that was believed to have existed during these times. It was thought that during the *sandai* sage kings ruled with wisdom, kindness, and compassion in a society of great harmony. The *sandai* as a model of a perfect society arose as early as the Eastern Zhou 东周 (770–256 BCE, the second phase of the Zhou Dynasty). Six exemplary kings of the *sandai*– Yao, Shun, Yu, Tang, Wen, and Wu (尧舜禹汤文武) – became venerated as legendary sages. Crucially, the *sandai* was admired by Confucius (551–479 BCE) who saw his own lifelong career merely as *shu er bu zuo* 述而不作 – explicating ancient wisdoms rather than creating new knowledge.

Throughout history, the romanticised *sandai* remained an archetypical model in the Confucian tradition: an eternal utopia in antiquity for all emperors to emulate. Using it as a standard, Confucian elites held the ruling dynasty accountable by comparing them to the sage kings of the *sandai* in the traditional *daotong* 道统 (tradition of the great *Dao*) – a Confucian moral order of which scholar-officials saw themselves as guardians. For the vast majority of Chinese society, this imagined classical perfection underpinned sociopolitical stability and the continuation of Chinese civilisation. In troubled times, the *sandai* acted as a beacon for court mandarins, guiding ruling dynasties through mishaps and hardships. The *sandai* is part of China's unique convention of 'revering antiquity' (*zun gu* 尊古) – a tradition of worshiping the classical age (pre-221 BCE) and its achievements. These achievements include the intellectual flourishing during the pivotal Spring and Autumn (770–476 BCE) and Warring States (475–221 BCE) periods when 'a hundred schools of thoughts contended' (*baijia zhengming* 百家争鸣), including Confucianism, Taoism, and Legalism. The *sandai* model is encapsulated in *datong* 大同 (great harmony) as a perfect society – an enduring utopia detailed in the Confucian classic *Liji* 礼记 (the Book of Rites) of the Warring States era. It envisages a world where *dadao* 大道 (the Great Way) prevails – everyone works for the collective; all are cared for, especially the weak; the moral and able rise to positions to govern; and trust and harmony triumph.

As China looked to its past for a perfect society, it also entertained a spatial utopian fantasy in the miniature world of '*shiwai taoyuan*' 世外桃源. *Shiwai taoyuan* was a pristine enclave of Confucian society set against an era of failed politics in the wider world. The hidden contemporaneous utopia compensated in the Chinese mind for the lost ideal of bygone days. The fantasy was created by the poet and scholar-official Tao Yuanming 陶渊明 (352–427 CE) in his celebrated *Taohuayuan Ji* 桃花源记 (An Account of Peach Flower Land). The poem describes the adventure of a fisherman who stumbles upon an idyllic village. Enchanted by the mesmerising beauty of a river valley, his curiosity takes him to a mountain cave that leads him to a hidden community – an unspoiled Confucian society cut off from the war-torn world for five centuries. As a primeval community of perfect harmony buried happily in history,[3] the *shiwai taoyuan* utopia met the same cultural ideal of social harmony and welfare for all. It is significant that the mythical dreamland is tucked away in the heart of the Chinese world (the story took place in what today is Hunan province). *Taoyuan* refers to a land of peach flowers; *shiwai* means 'hidden from the world'. It functioned as a criticism of the politics of the day and affirmed an ultimate faith in Confucian values that offer solutions to all social malaises. Its aspirations lay not in an exotic sociopolitical order in a fantasised foreign land like Thomas More's *Utopia*, but in an idealisation of a mundane, harmonious social life of the past.

This indigenous temporo-spatial utopia was maintained right up to the Self-Strengthening Movement that firmly upheld the cardinal '*hua–yi*' (Chinese vs barbarian) divide under the mantra of 'defeating the barbarians by learning from the barbarians' and 'Western learning as instruments and Chinese learning as essence'. It was not until 1895 that the Confucian dreamland began to crumble, when intellectual elites cast doubts on traditional values. For radical scholars like Liang, the 1895 reckoning swung their ideals swiftly to the counterworld of the West. Similarly, the temporal utopia reversed its direction – the backward-looking utopia turned to a forward-looking one. The future, however, points not only to an aspirational modernity modelled on the West, but to an antithesis of the past – a past once revered with pride came under intense scrutiny and increasing attack for its alleged failings. *Sandai* as a remedial exemplar for rectifying sociopolitical deviations fell quiet as the West rose as an exotic utopia for admiration and emulation. Much of traditional learning began to lose its weight and lustre as Chinese epistemology gave way to an alien one. This process, inaugurated by the 1895 defeat and 1898 abortive reform, sped up in the intellectual campaign against traditional norms.

In discussing utopia in modern Europe, Koselleck highlights its temporalisation, which he defines as a 'metamorphosis of utopia into the philosophy of history'.[4] That is to say, traditional utopias were spatial in externalising social ideals to a foreign land. But that started to change in the late eighteenth century with the onset of the 'future utopia'. The spatial counterworld thus turned into a temporal future world. What is significant is that this future world was imbued with the historical and even moral meaning of progress. Koselleck attributes the transformation from spatial to temporal utopia to the exhaustion of geographical exploration – Europeans had discovered all corners of the earth. Spatial fantasies, therefore, had to be transposed to the temporal 'unlimited future'. Nonetheless, Koselleck focuses only on utopia's *experiential* values. However, it is *social* values that underpin experiential values. The pre-modern spatial externalisation and modern temporalisation of utopia reflected Europe's historical curiosity about the outside world. But more importantly, it indicated modern (European) confidence in looking into the future. The onset of the 'future utopia' was driven by the extraordinary dynamics of social change and a new sense of power borne out of scientific and technological advances. In contrast, the Chinese antiquity-oriented internal utopia reveals an inward-looking and conservative mentality – a hallmark of a large agrarian society. Moreover, the *sandai* golden age and pre-Qin intellectual vibrancy are so deeply ingrained in the Chinese psyche that the gentry-scholar class were incapable of imagining anything better than ancient sages and classical learning.

The utopian reversal was instrumental to China's full-blown metamorphosis into a modern republic. It heralded stormy social upheavals because externalising and futurising utopia entailed a transformation of values that would be translated into rapid changes of sociopolitical institutions and practices. Ultimately, utopia functions as a way of articulating cherished values to rectify social problems. As Mannheim argues,[5] utopia represents not only a lack of congruity between perception and reality, but a consequential shattering of the social system. It is for this reason that Mannheim warns against the revolutionary nature of utopia that seeks to 'burst the bounds of the existing order'. The traditional *datong* ideal, however, provides only a temporary transition to a new system of values. Kang Youwei created a new theory, *datong sanshi shuo* 大同三世说 (great harmony through three ages), by combining the ancient *sanshi* 三世 (three ages) and *datong*. The reinterpreted Confucian concept was refashioned in a Western evolutionary vein for a unified vision of the future. Dressed in a Confucian cloak, Enlightenment values of democracy were highlighted as an effective basis on which to realise China's ancient dream of great harmony.

Liang was more specific in articulating a Confucian utopia in the context of Western progressive history. In his 1897 article 'On the Shift from the Rule by a King to the Rule by the People' in *Shiwu Bao* 时务报 (Journal of Current Affairs), *datong sanshi shuo* is transformed into 'democratic harmony'. The traditional three ages – disorder (*juluan-*

shi 据乱世), peace (*shengpingshi* 升平世), and harmony (*taipingshi* 太平世) – are re-presented as three stages of political governance: disorder under multiple rulers, peace under a single ruler, and harmony under democracy. The external utopia is thus cursorily re-internalised by repackaging it in an indigenous tradition. After the failed Hundred Days' Reform, the disillusioned Liang became increasingly drawn to Western learning. Chinese classics – the repertoire of values, inspirations, and spirituality – were drawn on with declining frequency. If referenced, it was not their values that were invoked for guidance as in the case of the *sandai*, but isolated wisdom of revered sages like Confucius, Mencius, Laozi, or Zhuangzi. Citing classics was reduced to a ritualistic, hollow homage to intellectual ancestors as emotive nostalgia. To Liang and his radical contemporaries, the traditional learning they had been nurtured in became a revered spiritual homeland that drifted away in its irrelevance to the modern world. The utopian impulse to reconfigure the 'conceptual map' as a new epistemological atlas for the world of tomorrow became irresistible.

CONCURRENT INTELLECTUAL AND LINGUISTIC TRANSFORMATIONS

Significant in the process of externalising utopia was an influx of Japanese loanwords into Chinese that provided the much-needed language for the intellectual campaign. Joseph Levenson calls the sudden rise of new words in the late Qing a 'new language' because 'this change of language in a society may be described objectively as new choices made under conditions of total invasion, not of purely intellectual insinuation.'[6] Previous loanwords in China's long history only enriched the Chinese vocabulary, but never altered the Chinese conceptual map. The shift from an 'enrichment of vocabulary' to a 'change in language' is part and parcel of the paradigmatic transformation of epistemology that came to dominate the intellectual scene. The inflow of loanwords in the critical decades from China's 1895 defeat in the First Sino-Japanese War to the 1919 May Fourth Movement was so extensive that over 70 percent of nouns in any modern Chinese political text are borrowed from abroad, mostly from Japan.[7] Matten calls these decades the 'threshold period' (*Sattelzeit*) from the perspective of conceptual history: when the political order shifted from Confucian universalism to the particularism of the nation-state.[8] The change of language in late Qing China is comparable to the German 'threshold period' of 1750–1850, when the German language changed into the language of modernity with the emergence of new concepts. But rather than being largely homegrown as in the case of Germany, the late Qing's 'new language' was predominantly imported, and in a rather short period of time. Unsurprisingly, these loanwords concentrate on concept nouns – the building blocks of a new episteme. Created in Meiji-era Japan (1868–1912), these concept nouns were largely coined by translating Western social science terms into (*kanji*) Japanese. Historically, Chinese was introduced to Japan over two thousand years ago and formed the basis of written Japanese. In what is called the 'Chinese character cultural sphere', East Asian societies share the same linguistic root in the Chinese script that helped spread Confucian cultural influence. Vandermeersch compares it to the Latin script that provided a repertoire for the formation of modern European languages.[9] However, the flow of linguistic and cultural influence was reversed in late Qing China, when Japanese loanwords facilitated a rapid Western cultural penetration into China. The fact that the graphic image of Chinese *hanzi* and Japanese *kanji* is identical complicates the notion of translation in its surreptitious transfer of Western ideas to China. The 'graphic loans' replaced the original sense of Chinese characters and imbued them with Western post-Enlightenment concepts and values.[10]

The new lexicon constructed a Western conceptual map in making sense of late Qing society. The map consisted not only of individual concepts but also determined the way they are incorporated into an intellectual structure organised and classified into complex relations. Central to the new language was a lexis of the nation-state and its constitutive institutions. Availing himself fully of a long exile in Japan from 1898 to 1912, Liang drew heavily from Japanese-language translations of Western social science texts, and he absorbed an enormous number of loanwords into his own writing. In *Xinmin Shuo*, eight of the ten most frequently occurring concepts are expressed in loanwords – *ziyou* 自由 (liberty), *quanli* 权利 (rights), *guomin* 国民 (*volk*), *sixiang* 思想 (thought), *guojia* 国家 (state), *zhuyi* 主义 ('-ism'), *yiwu*

义务 (obligation), and *minzu* 民族 (nation). Under each term is a cluster of related sub-concepts, again mostly in loanwords, that define its specific semantics. These eight words became macroconcepts that defined the epistemological structure, as well as delineated thematic foci of *Xinmin Shuo*.

The loanwords also contributed to the change of classical Chinese to modern Chinese. Key to lexical expansion was an upsurge of double-character (bisyllabic) words. Classical Chinese consists mostly of single-character (monosyllabic) words that had been used for over two millennia with stable meanings. This changed rapidly in the rise of modern Chinese – a vernacular that emerged at the beginning of the twentieth century. It is characterised by the predominance of double-character words. Combining characters with different denotations, a new semantics is created in the new word. Coined in Meiji Japan, many double-character terms were generated in translation, because they facilitated the rendition of unfamiliar ideas into *kanji* Japanese. For example, 'constitution' is translated as *xianfa* 憲法 in *kanji*. In classical Chinese, *fa* 法 means 'constant' and 'established institution'. *Xian* 憲 means the display of *fa* to people. *Xian* consists of three parts: the top 宀, representing rule; the middle 四, representing the eye; and the bottom 心, representing the heart. *Xian* means, therefore, that when a rule is displayed, one must observe it from the heart. By joining the two characters *xian* and *fa*, constitution as a Western institution was rendered in Japanese. But unlike 'constitution', a term that for something that takes a physical, codified form in written texts and which has specific institutional agencies for its enforcement, abstract nouns like 'nation' and 'liberty' are difficult to translate. Translating 'nation', for example, represented a major challenge as there were no historical experiences to draw on to make sense of the term. At least fifteen terms were used to translate 'nation' from the 1850s to the 1910s.[11]

The idea of the state is deceptively simple in translation. A comparable concept in Chinese is *guo* 国 – a feudal principality that existed before the Qin unification of China into a single civilisation in 221BC. Since then, *guo* as an independent political entity ceased to exist. Instead, it gained a new sense – an imperial court (*chaoting* 朝廷) presiding over the universal world of *tianxia* 天下 ('all under heaven'). *Tianxia* as a cultural concept represents a moral and cosmic order, in which the emperor rules as the 'son of heaven' with the 'mandate of heaven'. This sense of *guo* persisted until the Western notion of the state came to China in the late nineteenth century. 'State' is translated as *guojia* 国家, literally meaning 'state family'. Such a translation is easily understood within its traditional semantics as 'imperial court'. Adding *jia* (family) to *guo* only reinforces the weight of regal power. Historically, *jia* and *guo* have a similar structure with an authoritative figure as its head. Indeed, it is within this semantic frame that Zhang Deyi 张德彝 (1847–1918), a late Qing diplomatic interpreter, translated 'royal' in English as *guojia* in his 1887 diary of his travels to Europe. Guo Songtao 郭嵩焘 (1818–1891), the first Chinese ambassador to the UK, translated 'government' as *guojia*. Such confusions arose as the result of the loss of the intrinsic meaning of 'state' when translated as *guojia*. Loanwords, therefore, cannot guarantee the full transfer of the Western concepts they represent. These concepts need persistent interpretation, clarification, reiteration, and promotion for their meanings to be fully articulated and understood. This is the role Liang plays prominently in his national character-building campaign that focused on propagating Western ideas of the nation-state, though within his own rather slanted understanding, to guide social reform.

XINMIN AS A NATIONAL CHARACTER-BUILDING DRIVE

Liang's campaign is conventionally seen as conservative within modern Chinese historiography, due largely to his support for constitutional monarchy. His conservatism is contrasted with the revolutionary republicanism led by Sun Yat-sen, who saw no option but to topple the ethnically alien Manchu rule to modernise China. Liang's political conservatism was driven by his frustrations with the population's inertia in a period of national crisis. For him, the real obstacle to saving China lay in the prevalent *bumin* 部民 (tribal people) mentality. *Bumin* referred to the vast peasantry who cared only about their own close-knit clans and face-to-face communities. For Liang, it was this *bumin* mindset that made China feeble in the context of modern inter-state competition, because it divided China into millions of isolated communities. His campaign was designed to counter it by developing a sense of *qun* 群 – a larger community bound together by shared interests. By combining these *qun* as a commonwealth of public-minded people, Liang hoped to develop the ultimate *qun* in China – a Chinese nation. Indeed, it was Liang who coined the term 'Chinese nation' (*Zhonghua minzu* 中华民族) in 1902,[12] which became the most powerful term in twentieth-century China. A campaign on the mind, argued Liang, was more fundamental than a campaign on the polity. He attacked Sun Yat-sen's revolution as unwise and counterproductive. Without removing *bumin* attitudes, Liang argued, a political revolution would only bring bloodshed, chaos, and a worse form of dictatorship. Liang's political conservatism, nonetheless, conceals his intellectual ardour in engineering a mental transformation. Shifting from institutional reform to national character building, Liang created a *xinmin* discourse that stirred up a fervent response from young, idealistic, literate elites who identified with his frustrations, aspirations, and calls for 'mind reform' – a concept that was taken up later by both the Nationalist Party (Kuomintang) and the Communist Party of China in their programmes for remaking society.

Having studied Europe's rapid rise in the nineteenth century, Liang concluded that its success lay in a superior national character (*guominxing* 国民性). It was refined personal qualities that enabled individuals to rise above narrow self-interest and organise themselves into powerful nations through rational cooperation. It was the individual that made a nation great, he argued, not the other way round. Inter-state competition, in the final analysis, was a contest between the strength of individuals. This Darwinian view, popularised by Yan Fu's 严复 (1853–1921) translation of Thomas Huxley's *Evolution and Ethics*, was articulated in the inaugural article of *Xinmin Shuo*:

> A country is a congregation of people. People to a country are like the four limbs, five internal organs, ligaments, and blood vessels to the human body. When the limbs are broken, organs damaged, ligaments severed, and blood vessels ripped, the body will not survive. When people are ignorant, turbid, timid, weak, fragmented, and muddle-headed, the country will not survive. If one aspires to longevity, one needs to understand how to take care of his body. If a

> country aspires to security, wealth, respect, and prosperity, it needs to be well versed in knowing how to renew its people.[13]

Xinmin is a concept in the classical text *Da Xue* 大学 (Great Learning) that embodied the Confucian belief in good governance through moral cultivation and renovation of people. Traditionally, *min* refers to an unspecified collective in relation to the ruler. *Min* is conventionally understood as consisting of four hierarchical social strata: *shi* (scholars), *nong* (farmers), *gong* (artisans), and *shang* (merchants).[14] Scholars as the literati class dominated the social hierarchy, with *nong* as the vast peasantry coming next, and artisans and merchants residing at the bottom. By locating China's problems firmly in the unspecified population of *min*, Liang underlined the allegedly collective myopia to larger public interests. China's defective and debilitating national character was invisible in domestic politics but came to the fore when confronted with Western challenges. Despite China's enormous size, its strength was crippled by its inability to form a cohesive body for effective self-defence. To Liang, a new republic manned by parochial people would end up imploding into a new autocracy. Therefore, without breaking loose from the tenacity of a flawed national character, no real sociopolitical change would be possible. With such an assessment of society and reform rationale, Liang passionately promoted his 'new people' discourse in *Xinmin Shuo.*

However, *Xinmin Shuo* consists largely of an attack on national characters that he detailed in the twenty essays in *Xinmin Congbao.* Using his pen name 'Zhongguo zhi Xinmin' 中国之新民 (China's New Person), Liang describes China's sixteen entrenched but unexamined collective behavioural traits, ranging from temperament to disposition and mortality, that he claimed constituted China's unflattering national character. Each trait is dealt with in a full essay. They include: public morality, state consciousness, adventurous spirit, rights consciousness, liberty, self-governance, progress, self-respect, cooperation, profit-making and sharing, perseverance, obligations, warrior spirit, private moralities, collective morale, and political ability.[15] Invariably, the positive character traits he describes in these categories were assigned to Europeans and negative ones to Chinese.

Positive patterns of behaviour defined what he emphasised as *guomin* 国民 (nation people) – a Japanese translation of the German word *volk* based largely on the Swiss-German jurist and politician Johann Kaspar Bluntschli's (1808–1881) influential book *The Theory of the State*. For Liang, *guomin* was the model of his 'new people' – those who appreciate and fight for national interests.[16] Obviously, Liang wanted to transform Chinese *bumin* into European *guomin* in outlook, behaviour, and mindset. In a dichotomised portrayal, he assigned negative traits to Chinese parochial *bumin*. His 'new people', as 'nation people' akin to the *volk*, was intended to transmute a local communal identity to a national political identity by shifting their loyalty away from their clan-based face-to-face community to the nebulous 'nation' as an 'imagined community' of strangers.[17]

Contrary to earlier scholars who attempted to achieve epistemological congruence by locating Western learning in Chinese classics,[18] Liang chose to shake off such pretension in his open criticism of Chinese traditions. In fact, he followed the footsteps of Yan Fu – a leading thinker and translator of Western social science works – who was the first to break this mode of writing. With four powerful essays published in 1895, Yan had swept away the deceptive notion that everything intellectual was a product of China. However, the dilemma remained – should Chinese scholars accept the West as the source of ideas and ultimate knowledge? Liang opted for a partial conceptual evasion. He elevated Western knowledge to a canonical status without explicitly criticising Chinese intellectual tradition. Instead, he turned his attack to the social practice of everyday life. Such an attack is encapsulated in his well-known evaluation of China's problem as *renmin wanlie* 人民顽劣 (stubborn and narrow-minded people). Liang's *renmin wanlie* thesis originated in Yan Fu's essay 'On the Origins of [National] Strength'. Yan proposed to strengthen three types of power that China lacked – *minli* 民力 (physical power), *minzhi* 民智 (intellectual power), and *minde* 民德 (moral power). Yan highlighted moral power as in urgent need for improvement by curbing private interests that were detrimental to national interests. Liang refashioned Yan's 'moral character improvement' into national character-building as a necessary condition for nation building.

The new people discourse was, therefore, linked explicitly to nationalism: 'If we aspire to resist the national imperialism[19] of foreign powers and to save ourselves from annihilation, nationalism is the answer. If we aspire to nationalism, developing a new people is the approach.'[20] Liang's notion of *xinmin* as a 'new people' has been translated erroneously as 'new citizen' in most previous studies.[21] His notion of new people is not based on autonomous individuals seeking to protect their rights from the autocratic state; rather, people are asked to curb their self-interest to serve the nation-state. It represents Liang's approach to nation-building by moulding a new subjectivity of loyalty to the state. Instead of empowering the individual as a 'rights holder' in a Rousseauian sense, Liang underscored the state as a centre of the power and authority to organise national life. Liang's inspiration came largely from the state theory of Bluntschli, from whom Liang drew heavily in arguing for a strong state to replace the dynastic court. Liang was particularly attracted to Bluntschli's 'organic state' theory that advocates political collectivism. The organic state is seen as determining the outcomes of its organs – the people. Indeed, 'nation' was translated in the late Qing both as *minzu* 民族 (people's lineage) and *guomin*, among other terms. Liang chose *guomin* because this term underscored the critical importance of a 'people' who should have a good awareness of belonging to a 'nation', rather than to a traditional clan. *Minzu* and *guomin* in fact captured different aspects of 'nation'. *Minzu* focused on Chinese ethnicity, as emphasised by Sun Yat-sen in his political campaign to remove Manchu minority rule;[22] *guomin* was underlined by Liang for his cultural campaign to develop a new people.

FEATURES AND IMPACT OF *XINMIN SHUO*

The utopian *xinmin* discourse exerted an immediate impact on late Qing society in its call for radical social changes. Its influence has survived the late Qing and extends far into twentieth-century China. The *xinmin* discourse is characterised by a firm belief in the power of social engineering to achieve progress. Its daring, subversive spirit has reverberated throughout the revolutionary events of the twentieth century, moving in a linear and purposeful fashion towards an industrialist utopia. The power of utopia depends on a sense of idealism and can-do spirit, with no qualms about dismantling the deepest of traditions. Indeed, in *Xinmin Shuo* the most frequently occurring verb is *pohuai* 破坏 (destroy). Creation of the new may also mean the destruction of the old. There is little doubt in Liang's mind that the weight of China's long history was a liability. Nevertheless, the adventurousness, perseverance, and entrepreneurship that he called for are evident in China's post-reform economic development. However, it is the rejuvenation of the 'Chinese nation', the term Liang coined a century ago, that has taken off as the most enduring inspiration for Chinese people.[23] The dream of national revival has resonated as a powerful rallying call for unity, solidarity, and common purpose at times of crisis, just as the utopian *sandai* did in traditional China. The lure of utopia for a better world is as strong as ever.

A second aspect of *Xinmin Shuo* that keeps it relevant is its pragmatic attitude toward learning from the West. The *ti–yong* dichotomy framed the late Qing's two approaches to learning from the West. *Ti* 体 (essence) concerned fundamental values such as 'liberty' and 'rights' that set off immense controversy, whereas *yong* 用 (use) covered practical application of expertise such as technology and the market. *Ti* as a values system can be debated endlessly, but *yong* as approaches of getting things done was largely indisputable and far more favoured. It was, therefore, the practical *yong* that has taken the dominant role in China's modern transformation. Indeed, China's modernisation has been characterised by its capacity for perpetual appropriation. Except for the ideologically driven Cultural Revolution (1966–1976), dogmatic application of principle over practice is an aberration in modern China.

A final feature of the durability of *Xinmin Shuo* is statism. The 'new people' discourse bestows power unequivocally on the state. The power transfer from the emperor to the state constituted subtle continuities in post-imperial politics. *Xinmin Shuo* is conducive to the rise of statism in its persuasive promotion of the state as the centre of power, authority, loyalty, and the embodiment of the Chinese nation. The reified state has acquired an increased capacity to penetrate the society for bureaucratic control. The Bluntschlian organic state, combined with Hobbesian legitimacy and China's traditional moral authority, has created a mode of statehood that wields an unprecedented power. It has integrated horizontally legislative, administrative, and penal power, and vertically local, regional, and national power into a single centre of gravity that emits immense controlling influence nationwide. That concentration of power has bound the vast country together much more tightly than previous imperial dynasties. Related to statism is Liang's promotion of nation that has been integrated into the state as its core mission for development, revival, and prosperity. Evolving over a century, the state has inherited not only the traditional structure of polity but also a universalist mode of thinking which constitute key continuities from the past amidst severe ruptures, largely in terms of cultural values. The severed cultural tradition,[24] that Liang is in part responsible for, rests the nation on a narrow footing of ethnicity and race, resulting in a recurring misalignment between the state and nation. Modern China has therefore been viewed as an anomaly in the modern world of nation-states, described as 'a civilisation state'[25] or 'nationless state'.[26]

MODERN UTOPIANISM: BETWEEN EXTERNAL VALUES AND DOMESTIC REALITIES

Liang's utopian vision of society is constrained by the historical conditions of his time. The collective anxiety over the perception of an imminent national collapse is impossible to escape. The severity of the possible demise of the Chinese cultural order triggered a deep self-doubt that resulted in self-negation. European ideas adopted in such circumstances were inevitably prone to utopianism not only because they failed to appreciate Chinese conditions, but also because those who adopted them lacked knowledge about Europe. Aside from a handful of people who studied in the West, such as Yan Fu, most late Qing intellectuals gained their knowledge from limited secondary sources, mostly in or through Japan. The desire to emulate Europe arose, therefore, not as the result of a careful study but as a reflex to the disaster of the 1895 defeat and despair over the hopeless Manchu rulers seen as foreign to the Han Chinese. Mannheim attributes utopian thinking to exaggerated situations among disempowered groups who are so passionate to transform their conditions that they see only the elements that negate those conditions.[27] Motivated by a desire for immediate action, utopian thinking is susceptible to tunnel vision and false diagnoses of social problems.

What is missing from Liang's sweeping criticism of national character is an examination of China's historical conditions that gave rise to the alleged *bumin* behaviours. Liang failed to account for the alignment between the family-based mode of agricultural production and the *bumin* mentality. Agrarian China was shaped by social customs suited to clan-based communities unrelated to one another in a vast empire. Remotely linked to the *tianxia* order imagined by the literati and imperial court, millions of self-governing communities evolved organically into a social equilibrium with their own internal governance structure, norms, and ethics. Unlike European societies which were compelled to be organised into nation-states by the forces of modern commerce and warfare,[28] there were no internal dynamics of change to alter the Chinese social equilibrium. These were instead dictated by the imperative of an agricultural cycle of production that people's livelihood solely depended upon. By assessing the Chinese practice not in its environmental and sociohistorical conditions, but against a European model, Liang promoted a novel mode of state that combined traditional top-down authority with bottom-up obligation-bound popular participation. The fusion of imperial bureaucracy as a new state apparatus with an unprecedented societal penetration helped lay the foundation of modern Chinese politics. On this account, the journalist Liang reveals an intellectual deficiency as a serious thinker that Yan Fu had rightly accused him of. Despite this, Liang proved ultimately to be an effective purveyor of Western ideas and a sharp observer of the symptoms of China's political inertia. His intellectual radicalism nonetheless matches Sun Yat-sen's political radicalism, though it runs far deeper in China's modern consciousness throughout the twentieth century.

Nonetheless, as a gifted polemist, Liang avails himself of his powerful rhetoric and emotive language. His insurrectionary writings spread like wildfire in overseas Chinese communities and major urban centres in China. His elegant style and burning passion helped augment his message. Despite his unpopular advocacy for 'enlightened absolutism' as transition to a constitutional monarchy,

Liang's analysis of national characters exerted a lasting impact on young generations of Chinese in early-twentieth-century China – many of whom embraced change and took Liang as their guiding light. The historian Huang Zunxian remarked: 'Not a single May Fourth leader was untouched by Liang Qichao's writing.'[29] Even a young Mao Zedong was inspired to launch the New People Society (Xinmin Xuehui 新民学会) to emulate Liang's social reform, after reading *Xinmin Shuo* at the age of sixteen. Though constantly shifting positions, Liang is consistent in his support for a strong centralised state and identifies China's problem as the weaknesses of its people. Despite being labelled a conservative, he is far more subversive than currently acknowledged. If Sun Yat-sen is the father of revolution in a political sense, Liang is the father of revolution in a cultural sense. In his ardent pursuit of national character reform, Liang called for a series of revolutions – a 'revolution of poetry' (1899), 'revolution of novels' (1902), 'revolution of morals' (1902), and 'revolution of historiography' (1902). All were launched as preparations for creating a 'new people' – people reborn with a modern psyche, as well as superior mental and physical power. It is his concern with national building of character that sets Liang apart from revolutionaries who sought to establish a new republic and from traditionalists bent on the resurrection of Chinese culture for national survival, revival, and ultimate pre-eminence. Liang can be credited with enduring utopian idealism, cultural boldness, practical appropriation of Western ideas and arguing for a strong centralised state. Idealist and pragmatist, Liang was a powerful moderniser for whom the vision of utopia in China never faded.

NOTES

1. See, for example, the following studies: Joseph R. Levenson, *Liang Ch'i-ch'ao and the Mind of Modern China* (Cambridge, MA: Harvard University Press, 1953); Philip C. Huang, *Liang Ch'i-ch'ao and the Modern Chinese Liberalism* (Seattle: University of Washington Press, 1972); Xiaobing Tang, *Global Space and the Nationalist Discourse of Modernity: The Historical Thinking of Liang Qichao* (Stanford, CA: Stanford University Press, 1996).

2. Karl Mannheim, *Ideology and Utopia: An Introduction to the Sociology of Knowledge* (London: Routledge & Kegan Paul, 1954).
3. Upon the fisherman's reluctant departure, the villagers insist he tell no one about the village's existence. The fisherman, in his excitement, rushes to report to the local official who dispatches an investigation team but never finds the village. The idyllic Confucian utopia was forever locked in the Chinese imagination.
4. Reinhart Koselleck, *The Practice of Conceptual History: Timing History, Spacing Concepts* (Stanford, CA: Stanford University Press, 2002), 85.
5. Mannheim, *Ideology and Utopia*, 173.
6. Joseph R. Levenson, *Confucian China and Its Modern Fate: A Trilogy* (Berkeley: University of California Press, 1968), 159.
7. Wang Li, *Hanyu Shigao* [A history of the Chinese language] (Beijing: Zhonghua shuju, 1980), 516.
8. Martin Matten, '"China is the China of the Chinese": The Concept of Nation and Its Impact on Political Thinking in Modern China', *Oriens Extremus* 51 (2012): 97.
9. Leon Vandermeersch, *Le Nouveau Monde Sinise* (Paris: You Feng, 2004).
10. Joshua Fogel, ed., *The Role of Japan in Liang Qichao's Introduction of Modern Western Civilisation to China*, China Research Monographs, no. 57 (Berkeley, CA: Institute of East Asian Studies, University of California, 2004).
11. Matten, 'China is the China of the Chinese', 72.
12. Liang first used the term 'China nation' (*Zhongguo minzu* 中国民族) in 1901, but changed it to 'Chinese nation' in 1902, which became the dominant term ever since.
13. Liang Qichao, *Xinmin Shuo* [On new people] (Beijing: Zhongguo wenshi chubanshe, 2013), 3. Unless otherwise indicated, all translations of Liang's work are the author's own.
14. Such social stratification occurred during the Warring States period, as described in the Confucian classic *Guliang Zhuan* 谷梁传 that chronicled the history of the Warring States period, although *Guliang Zhuan* was only written in the Eastern Han Dynasty (25–220 CE). The explanatory note in the book defines the four social strata as 'scholars enjoying high status due to their superior virtues; farmers creating and farmland; artisans making utensils with their ingenuity and hands; and merchants facilitating the flow of finance and goods'.
15. These are the final sixteen chapters. The first four chapters are titled: (1) Outlines, (2) People Renewal as China's Most Urgent Task, (3)

Explaining People Renewal, and (4) People Renewal Effect Proved by the Survival of the Fittest Principles and Strategies of Renewal.

16. Qing Cao, 'A Corpus-Based Investigation of *Guomin*', *Journal of Chinese Sociolinguistics* 31 (2): 13–28.
17. Benedict Anderson, *Imagined Communities: Reflections on the Origin and Spread of Nationalism* (London: Verso, 1983).
18. Ying-shih Yu, 'The Radicalisation of China in the Twentieth Century', *Daedalus* 122 (2) (1993): 125–150.
19. Liang believed that excessive nationalism was imperialism.
20. Liang Qichao, *Xinmin Shuo*, 12.
21. Hao Chang, *Liang Ch'i-ch'ao and Intellectual Transition in China* (Cambridge, MA: Harvard University Press, 1971); Theresa Man Ling Lee, 'Liang Qichao and the Meaning of Citizenship: Then and Now', *History of Political Thought* 28 (2) (2007): 305–327; Hazama Naoki, 'On Liang Qichao's Conception of *Gong* and *Si*: "Civic virtue" and "Personal Virtue" in *Xinmin Shuo*', in Joshua A Fogel, ed., *The Role of Japan in Liang Qichao's Introduction of Modern Western Civilisation to China* (Berkeley, CA: Institute of East Asian Studies, University of California, 2004), 202–221; Zhonghua Guo, 'Translating Chinese Citizenship', in Engin F. Isin and Peter Nyers, eds., *Routledge Handbook of Global Citizenship Studies* (London: Routledge, 2004), 366–375.
22. Following the successful 1911 Xinhai Revolution, Sun changed his stance on nationality issues, and advocated a multi-ethnic 'Chinese nation' that included the Manchus, Mongols, Hui, and Tibetans.
23. Qing Cao, 'Discursive Construction of National and Political Identities in China', in Chris Shei, ed., *The Routledge Handbook of Chinese Discourse Analysis* (London: Routledge, 2019), 431–443.
24. Qing Cao, 'Rupture of Modernity: A Case Study of Radicalism in the Late Qing Chinese Press Debate', *Critical Arts: South-North Cultural and Media Studies* 31 (6) (2017): 9–28.
25. Lucian Pye, *The Spirit of Chinese Politics* (Cambridge, MA: Harvard University Press, 1992).
26. John Fitzgerald, 'The Nationless State: The Search for a Nation in Modern Chinese Nationalism', *Australian Journal of Chinese Affairs* 33 (1995): 75–104.
27. Mannheim, *Ideology and Utopia*, 36.
28. David Held, 'The Development of the Modern State', in Stuart Hall and Bram Gieben, eds., *Formations of Modernity* (Cambridge: Polity Press, 1992), 71–125.

29. The May Fourth Movement was a cultural and political campaign from the mid-1910s to the early 1920s that criticised Chinese cultural traditions and advocated Western science and culture. It was also an anti-imperialist nationalist campaign as a response to the 1919 Paris Peace Treaty.

2
Utopian Future in Chinese Poetry: Bian Zhilin in Republican China

Yang Zhou

Since the start of the twentieth century, utopian thinking has played a significant role in shaping China's political and cultural modernity. Chinese intellectuals were driven into a 'love-hate' relationship with Chinese traditions – they took pride in China's high culture but loathed the corrupt court and its hapless inertia at a time of national crisis. They were equally ambivalent about the West – their moral outrage over Western colonialism in China was matched only by their passionate embrace of Western values and institutions in a desperate attempt to find a 'magic wand' to cure China's perceived ills. This double ambivalence created a distinct mode of thinking and expression in imagining a modernist future during the Republican period (1911–1949).

This chapter examines the modernist aesthetic formation in the New Poetry Movement through its most representative figure – poet, translator, and literary scholar Bian Zhilin卞之琳 (1910–2000).[1] There is a specific focus on his work between 1930 and 1937, namely his 'pre-war poetry', with reference to his other works in prose and articles reviewing his own literary practice. I intend to show the connection between the poet Bian Zhilin's professed association with French symbolist poetry and his much deeper connection with classical Chinese poetics. Beyond textual analysis I refer to Bian's translation works and the arguments of Chinese intellectuals during Bian's active period to draw a comparison between French symbolist poetry and Bian's own poetics. By examining, at the same time, the private symbols in Bian's pre-war poetry and revealing the resources of the poet's emotional structure, rather than lingering on the customary discussions of the construction of Westernised modernity, fresh insight into Bian's poetry can be gained. Bian's Westernised modernity has much to do with an imagined ideal that accommodates the poet's yearning for tradition, but the artistic agency comes from classical Chinese poetry. Therefore, Bian's pre-war poetry, despite its birthmarks from symbolism and metaphysical poetry, can be recognised as a Chinese child.

Bian's experiment with articulating a modern social critique in emulating French symbolism reveals his nostalgic longing for the lyrical beauty of Chinese classical poetry. French symbolism and metaphysical poetry paradoxically serve as a bridge between Bian's desire to fashion a modernist, 'progressive' aesthetic and his subconscious return to his spiritual home in Chinese classics. This double ambivalence is symptomatic of the complex feelings of anxiety, doubt, and hope of Chinese cultural elites in the period. The denial of the Chinese reality coupled with the romantic imagining of a modern West had the power to produce a belief in a bright Chinese future of aesthetic modernity that evaporated in post-war China.

MODERNISATION AND UTOPIA IN CHINESE POETRY IN THE 1930S AND 1940S

China has long been fascinated by modernity, but the Chinese notion of modernity has proven difficult to define. The May Fourth period (1915–1921), with its combination of political, cultural, and social radicalism, is perceived by many intellectuals as the fountainhead of Chinese modernity. This idea has inevitably been connected to the notion of the West, as well as the idea of progress presented to China, deemed by many concurrent intellectuals as the 'sleeping giant' despite internal and external crisis in the early twentieth century. An omnipresent eagerness from the assumption of a 'belated modernity'[2] dominated China's quest for modernity and resulted in the recognition of a bright future through modernisation that would at least match China with the West. Modernity, therefore, is treated as a historical task of collective efforts. Put against such a historical context, modernity in Chinese literature has inevitably been studied as an accompaniment of drastic socioeconomic struggle and progress. At the start of the New Culture Movement, modernity in Chinese literature was reflected, first of all, in a revolution concerning the form of writing, including *Baihua* (vernacular Chinese) in contrast to classical Chinese, the written standard used during imperial China to the early twentieth century. Writing in vernacular Chinese validated intellectuals' common pursuit of new and free writing styles opposed to classical Chinese literature. The rise, as well as the prosperous development, of fiction writing extended to today is considered by many modern scholars to be the most remarkable symbol of modernity in literature.[3] At the same time, lyricism, with its focus on individual expressions of emotions and appreciation of beauty, seems to be 'exiled'. However, instead of being marginalized, lyricism established a dialogue with the eagerness for political transformation, thus actively participating in the quest for modernity by raising the question of 'How should an individual feel and express him/herself in modern China?' Works of the late Crescent Moon Society poets contain aesthetic aspects both of Western romanticist and symbolist poetry and of classical Chinese poetry of contemplation and Taoist morality and aestheticism.

Ban Wang demonstrated how politics in modern China has been closely intertwined with an aesthetic experience that is defined by its function for collective social purposes.[4] It is then no surprise that any attempt towards the beautiful and towards emotions free from ideology and socialist culture – such as the poetry of the Crescent Moon Society – would be seen as bourgeois and false.

Leo Ou-fan Lee pointed out three 'imperative and inevitable' major variations of modern Chinese literature, all constrained by the historical perspective. First, the moral vision of China as a diseased nation created a sharp polarity between tradition and modernity, defining modernity as 'an iconoclastic revolt against this tradition and an intellectual quest for new solutions'. Second, modern literature became a vehicle wherein social discontent was expressed by writers; therefore, literature itself acquired its modernity, not through 'spiritual or artistic considerations (as in Western modernistic literature)', but through a sociopolitical stance. Third, as modern Chinese literature reflects an overpowering sense of sociopolitical anguish, writers offered a subjective critical vision where the writer's narratives are seen as opposed to the ill society, which 'thus gives rise to an aggravated ambivalence in the modern Chinese writer's conception of self and society'.[5] Lee again noted that this ambivalence has caused a subjective tension, where writers hope for a better future, a historical goal, which caused at the same time a feeling of disgust with the present reality. This subjective tension might serve an underlying motivation for literary creativity since early-twentieth-century China. However, such a literary creativity deviated greatly from Western modernist literature in its ambivalence in conceptualising individualism and exploring the self,

As students and ambassadors bearing witness to modern Europe, Chinese poets active between the 1930s and 1940s fell into the pursuit of a perfect continent that they could easily locate on the world map. Therefore, the motivation for bringing back this temporal utopia, or at least, maintaining the experience and feelings they had had in that utopia, is part of their motivation for modernising lyricism. The case of Hu Shi and his followers' belief in social Darwinism in literature is a reflection of this utopian vision, which also caused the assumption of 'belated modernity' in China and the political eagerness simply to catch up – 'a certain patriotic provinciality and a naiveté of faith with regard to better conditions elsewhere'.[6]

When New Poetry was at its beginning, Xu stated, 'the Crescent Moon is hanging in the sky, though not a symbol of a sweeping power. Its thin crescent is implying the full accomplishment of a bright future'.[7] This promise of a bright future was negated by the Second Sino-Japanese War.

SYMBOLISM AND CLASSICAL CHINESE POETRY

If we consider Bian's situation in 1934, we can understand why the poet feels so restless in his mind despite his identity as a philosopher. The comparison between mind and body is not unlike the comparison between 'a few memories of the past three years' and 'the taste of new autumn', as the former is bitter and hopeless to a poet trapped in 'Peking, 1934'. Bian describes himself from 1930 to 1934 as restless and exhausted: he 'could not find peace' and 'could not find my rest'.[8]

As an attempt to find the resolution, not unlike his literary peers such as Dai Wangshu and Yu Dafu, Bian Zhilin began his practice of emulating Western poetic styles in English romanticism and French symbolist poetry with the formal qualities of poems. Bian's translation of Valéry's work kept strictly to the rhyme-and-stanza scheme of the original, developing some lively rhythms within the compass of its short, spare lines. Bian's translation techniques have contributed much to this successful emulation of rhymes and meters in poems including 'The White Shell', 'Song', 'Sea Sorrow', and 'A Piece of Broken Ship'. The musical qualities shared by both the *Book of Odes* and most poems written by Paul Verlaine may have laid the literal foundation for the possible similarities between classical Chinese and symbolist poetry. However, looking beyond formal qualities, it is not difficult to understand that Bian's understanding of symbols and their expressions is closely related to the Chinese tradition shaped by literati poetry in the Tang and Song Dynasties.

According to Bian's comments in *Window on the West* and his 1980s monologue in *Poems of Ten Years*, intimacy and suggestion are the two 'old friends' that led him to the path of writing as a symbolist. In his 1921 book *Paul Verlaine*, Nicolson offered his dispassionate praise for the poet in the final chapter, 'Verlaine's Literary Position', which contains a number of passages of striking relevance to Bian's own poetry. Nicolson described symbolism as inseparable from the features of 'intimacy' and 'suggestion', these being 'the two essential qualities which raise true lyric poetry above the level of merely elegiac'.[9] In Nicolson's presentation, 'intimacy' implied

> A feeling of a definite and immensely human personality. . . . Its effect resides firstly in the sparing and skillful use of attributes, in an apparently incidental but vivid reference to minor objects which . . . radiate with emotional significance. It is not that such objects are themselves of any interest . . . it is simply that our sentiment of association is set vibrating by these references, that a pleasurable chord is struck by the thought of other objects, intimate to us, which have precisely such a connexion in our own experience.[10]

Bian Zhilin described his strategy as inspired by Nicolson's ideas of symbolism by using the verb *jie*借 (borrow): 'I express by borrowing emotions from natural sceneries, objects, other people and their business'.[11] In his pre-war poetry, emotion relies heavily on affective images. Expression of feelings is usually carried out by a centralized yet implicit 'I' in the poem, to uplift the emotion of the writer. Bian's style of writing has received much praise in China due to this seemingly close affiliation to symbolist and modernist poetry.

Bian's poetry was greatly admired by the Chinese literary critic Fei Ming (1901–1967), who wrote in his celebrated lecture series in Peking University about New Poetry that he especially admired Bian's combination of the modern and the traditional: 'his literary style is most modern; his taste is, however, the most traditional'. Tang Qi (1920–1990), the representative figure of the 'Nine Leaves' poets in the 1940s, also wrote the following in his essay 'Bian Zhilin and Modernist Poetry':

> Bian has absorbed the influence from the French symbolists and the modernists from England and America; with which, at the same time, he assimilated traditional Chinese philosophies and artistic creativity. He has developed a new path and crystalized his unique poetics.[12]

The path, however, may not be as 'new' as Bian and his critics had hoped. Bian's strategy is as similar to the classical Chinese concept of *xing* 兴 as to his claimed Western affinities, if not more so. Bian's good friend Liang Zongdai, a well-known Chinese disciple of Valéry, introduced Bian, a student in Peking University in 1920s, to French symbolism. Liang was among the very few Chinese intellectuals that attempted to compare the association and sense of finality described by Nicolson with the strategy of *xing* in classical Chinese literature. In fifth-century classical Chinese text on literary theory, *Wen Xin Diao Long*文心雕龙 (The Literary Mind and the Carving of Dragons), *xing* was referred to as a literary strategy: 'those who intend to express emotions must start by exploring significance in minor objects'. Liang talks about the relevance of *xing* by defining symbolism as 'an imprint of our feelings on that piece of scenery'.[13] Liang cited the Song

Dynasty book of literary theory *Xu Jinzhen Shige* 续金针诗格 (Golden Needle: Rules of Poetry Continued) to explain the strategy of symbolizing: 'A poem should always carry with it two layers of meanings: the internal layer intended as an expression of emotions and ideas; and the external layer of depicting its symbols. A poem is not fit for appreciation unless both its layers are written in an implicit style.'[14]

Many of Bian's pre-war poems respond to the two layers of meaning: 'New Autumn' incorporates a light-hearted description of the season and implied sadness over lost love though no direct mention of love can be traced; 'Round Treasure Box' relies on the symbol of a bridge to connect the past and the future, implying the poet's own idealism flowing down the river of life; 'Fragment', on the other hand, though written in simple, short words, buries an endless story of sadness underneath the poetic air of carelessness.

A good example is the image of autumn and the setting sun in Bian's pre-war poetry, as he expresses two layers of solitude: physical isolation and the deeper, Confucian solitude on the metaphysical level, as explored by the Tang Dynasty poet Du Fu and Song Dynasty poet Lu You. In the first half of 'Shadows' (1931), the images are presented in an 'obviously classical Chinese ambience';[15] an overwhelming feeling of solitude is projected in the image of sunset that lengthens shadow. This style could be traced back to Lu You, who projects his sorrow and desperation in the words 'My lonely sorrow in the time of sunset, added by the wind and the rain' (*yi shi huanghun duzi chou, gengzhe feng he yu* 已是黄昏独自愁, 更著风和雨), which express the feelings of a poet from a defeated nation.

The second half of 'Shadows' shifts the subjective emotion into a scene of the special relationship between the shadow and the subject. Compared to the first half, where parallel images of solitude and weariness create the ambience that resembles those in classical Chinese poetry, the second half of 'Shadows' is apparently more important, since it has elevated and deepened the feelings projected on images through a scene with dramatic qualities. The consolation provided by the shadow is accentuated through, first, the separation between the man and his shadow: the shadow is described as a friend to 'me', which is sent by a second person ('you'); and, second, through the dramatic switch from the first half of symbolist expression of subjective emotion to a scene of 'me' talking to both the shadow and the imagined friend from afar, whose whereabouts are unknown. Identities are shared not only by the shadow and 'you', but also by the poet and 'you'. In fact, the shadow itself could also be seen as the poet himself. Solitude in the first half of the poem is transformed into a metaphysical solitude in which 'I' can communicate with the self and reflect upon the feeling of solitude. Therefore, the conversation amongst the two persons and the shadow has an extraordinary emotional effect. The theme of metaphysical solitude is again emphasised as readers come to understand that 'I', 'you', and the shadow are all poetic avatars of the poet himself.

In his 1980s monologue in *Poems of Ten Years*, half a century after his most fruitful years as a poet, Bian confesses his preference for late Tang Dynasty poetry, revealing the identity of the 'old friend' that he met when reading about intimacy and suggestion in symbolism. Expressing emotions between 'turning loose' and 'escape',[16] Jiang Kui, one of the three Tang poets named by Bian Zhilin, was a representative figure in imprinting his emotions on minor surroundings through a hidden self. Hiding his experience and feelings behind words, it was a common practice for Jiang Kui and his contemporary poets including Li Shangyin and Du Mu to start from a point, either in time or in geography, to develop a full poem composed with a shadow of experience through description of a minor scenery followed by an implicit expression of feelings. For example, the city of Huainan has been employed in ten different poems by Jiang Kui, where the hidden self in the poem observes details such as the 'clear wind and moon over a small boat riding the gentle waves' ('Shadow of Prunus Blossoms from the Sky') and 'the bright moonlight [which] kept the thousand mountains cold' ('Strides Over Silk'). The poet's emotions are reflected in detailed observation of minor surroundings such as the depiction of leaving his homeland and a recollection of a long goodbye from a lover.

In 1935, Bian's friend, the poet Li Jianwu, published his review of Bian Zhilin's second poem collection, *Fish Eyes* (1935), and passionately appraised it as follows:

> The modernity of Bian, who represents a minority of poets in the front line of writing as a modern man, lies in the suggestion of symbols organised in a strict stanza that is intended to maintain a vague dream in which the unlimited beauty of poetry could be seen through limited mortal eyes.[17]

However, Bian strongly disagreed with Li's analysis of 'Fragment'. Li sees the sorrow in 'Fragment' as 'the poet's views over life: nothing in life is beyond the function of decoration' and argues that despite the sad internal layer of meaning, the poem is beautiful due to the poet's focus on decoration in the art of poetry. Bian published an article in response to Li's review: 'I emphasize on the relativity of symbols (in the space created in "Fragment")'.[18] This active public rejection of a friend's passionate article of praise is proof of this shy, low-key poet's strong belief in his poetic ideals. As a matter of fact, relativity has played a central role in many of Bian's pre-war poems, such as 'Chi Ba', 'Round Treasure Box', and 'Sail'. These poems, through simple words and short verses, create a space of imagination where the poet's emotions and thoughts are so implicit that they are mere traces. 'The Composition of the Distances', written in 1935, is one of the most frequently discussed poems of Bian. Relativity of symbols plays the role of the central theme of this poem and a closer examination reveals the poet's close relationship to classical Taoist philosophy.

The title 'The Composition of the Distances' involves the use of images from classical Chinese literature and others introduced from life in modern society and influences from the West. These are threaded together by thoughts of the persona; as 'I' lets his thoughts free, distances between times and spaces continually change, intensifying the overlap of *xu* 虚 (reflection) and *shi* 实 (location). For example:

> When I dream of reading alone on the highest terrace
> 'The Decline and Fall of the Roman Empire'
> there appeared in the newspaper the star that marks the Fall.
> The newspaper drops on the floor. The atlas opens
> to a thought travelling to a far-off name.
> The landscape received here is now clouded with twilight . . .

There are also allusions in classical Chinese literature and philosophy:

> How tired! No one really stirred the boat in my basin,
> no one caused a storm in the sea?

In the last two lines, the exhaustion and feelings of being lost in one's imagination are replaced by an experience in reality:

> O my friend has brought me five o'clock
> and the sign of impending snow.[19]

DEPERSONALIZATION AND CLASSICAL CHINESE AESTHETICS

Bian's writings in 1930 evidence the dislocation of the period. His imagination of modernity is limited to emulation of Western form and superficial style. It would be fair to say that modernity in Bian's pre-war poetry exists only in the vernacular and formal quality. Bian himself felt highly uncomfortable in his poetic pursuit and said, 'whenever I wrote a poem, I feel like my body was lost in a deep valley, though my mind was striving to speak from the peak of the mountain above'.[20] Bian also wrote about his lack of confidence and the fear of standing out in a crowd: 'I would rather hide my face.'[21] The rift is between a mindset to write according to 'that Western school' and a body suffering the despair of a Chinese man, not so different from that of Qu Yuan in the Warring States period (475–221 BCE) and Du Fu in the Tang Dynasty, whose heart was broken by the An Lushan Rebellion of 755 CE.

In an article about the Crescent Moon Society's representative figure, Wen Yiduo, Bian attributed this change of his writing to T. S. Eliot:

> My 'techniques' in poetry writing, apart from what I learnt from classical Chinese poetry and the West, most of them are from nowhere but 'the Dead Water'! For example, I tend to write a dramatic scene, a dramatic monologue or conversation when writing a poem; I'd even write a poem in the style of writing a novel.[22]

Bian explained the technique as a result of the teaching of the Crescent Moon Society. However, in playing the role of a catalyst that allows free feelings to enter into new combinations, Bian constructs also a perspective towards beauty and emotions that is highly valued in classical Chinese poetry.

The writing strategy of Jiang Kui, much admired by Bian, represents a common practice of incorporating Taoist aesthetics of 'viewing objects from the eyes of the object' (*yi wu guan wu* 以物观物) and the impersonal state (*wuwo zhi jing* 无我之境) of writing where emotions of the 'I' are no longer the centre of the poet's response to his surroundings. According to Wang Guowei, a versatile scholar of classical Chinese aesthetics in the late Qing Dynasty, when self-consciousness is placed in the centre, 'in the personalized state [*youwo zhi jing*有我之境] the poet views objects in terms of himself so everything takes on his colouring'.[23] Wang sees the other state, where self-consciousness is 'hidden as a secondary viewer', as arguably successful in its value of art and beauty. In the impersonal state of writing, 'The poet views objects in terms of the objects; we cannot tell if the poet is himself, or has he immersed into the state of the object. Most ancient poets write in the personal state. However, that is not to say that they have not been able to reach the impersonal state; but to do so takes an unrestrained, brave soul of classical Chinese literati that stands completely on his own.'[24]

Bian wrote about his tendency of hiding the 'I' in his poetic writing as follows: 'Poets are "animals of emotions". When I write poems, though they are all lyrical, I tend to control myself from indulging my feelings, as if I'd prefer to be "cold blooded". . . . I filter my words and thoughts; I long for when my poems rise above myself and crystalize.'[25] It is not just the poet's personality that drives him to weaken his subjective feelings. Influences from post-symbolism, and more importantly, classical Chinese poetry, are key to his transformation from his predecessors' writings about prevalent images such as dreams, roses, and tears, serving the sole goal of free expression of superficial emotions.

Bian used the word *yijing* 意境 (meaning and ambience), a term in classical Chinese art, to explain his strategy of parody and depersonalization. For Bian, the purpose of the decentralized 'I' in a poem is that of creating a proper ambience, or *yijing*, so that the poem could be read and understood beyond its words, an idea that he links to the strategy of suggestion in symbolism. About the importance of 'suggestion', Nicolson declared that for the symbolists 'the fatal thing in creation was a sense of finality: the masterpiece should begin only where it appeared to end; it should not merely describe, it should suggest; it should leave behind it some unexpressed vibration. It is . . . indication of the unattained'.[26] In Bian's poems, the strategy is realized through what the poet called 'crystallization'; relativity, as shown in 'Fragment', is frequently used to create endless meanings which depend on the reader's interpretation. Crystallization also corresponds to the effect of *wuqiong* 无穷 (endless meaning) in classical Chinese literature. *Wuqiong* originates in the teachings of Buddhism. At the same time, due to the nature of the effect, classical Chinese plays and stories usually write between illusion and reality in order to achieve this effect for the readers.

Bian reflects on his pre-war poetry, saying that 'some sing the tone of "Fin de Siecle" from the West whilst some play melodies from late Tang Dynasty and the Southern Song'.[27] The structure and allusions of 'The Composition of Distances' shows how the poet pieces together these strategies into a poem of his own.

Seven footnotes followed this poem, ten lines in its original language. According to the poet, he read in the newspaper about the discovery of a supernova, the bright light of which was caused by 'an explosion during the time of the Roman Empire'. Therefore, the first three lines point to the relativity of time, a topic that appeared repeatedly in Bian's pre-war poetry. The poem is written in the structure of classical Chinese play and the poet emphasized in his notes that 'this is not a poem of any mysterious philosophy of my own thoughts; instead, it is about a certain type of feelings set in a certain type of *yijing*'.

The 'certain type of *yijing*' resembles that of the Eastern Jin and Liu Song Dynasty poet Tao Yuanming's famous poem 'Drinking Wine', which includes the following lines:

> Picking chrysanthemums under the eastern fence,
> One pensively views the southern mountains.

The mountain air and sunset are beautiful;
Flying birds return together.
There is true meaning in this;
Desiring argument, one stops and forgets to speak.[28]

Yan Canglang, a literature scholar in the Song Dynasty, highly admired Tao's poem because it 'contains a natural poetic quality that surpasses exquisite artifacts (in Xie Lingyun's poem of a similar idyllic theme)'.[29] The reason why a poet's exquisite techniques in making metaphors (as in Xie's other poem) are inferior to the 'natural poetic quality' lies in the inexhaustible meaning, *wuqiong*. In 'Drinking Wine', the poet leads an idyllic life, away from orthodoxy among the literati, immersed in the pensive view of the southern mountain in sunset. The identity of the poet is therefore engaged in a dynamic relative to that of his surroundings. The 'true meaning' in this relativity, according to the poet himself, cannot be comprehended through mere words. Instead, the reader gets involved with the relativity and therefore associated with the unstated 'true meaning'. Therefore, when reading 'Drinking Wine', one is drawn, not only to the idyllic scenery, but also to *wuqiong* behind the closely associated symbols.

The Chinese intellectuals during and after the May Fourth Movement avidly embraced the Western tradition with practically no understanding of what it had meant to the West. This was due to the fact that China had hardly any experience of industrialization, and therefore knew nothing about the threats posed by modernity: reification of the natural self. The only motivation of China's embrace of the Western idea of self lies in the coveted social order of democracy and liberalism.

However, the combined native and foreign aggression had, since the 1920s, driven the Chinese intellectuals into the simultaneous love and hate for Chinese and Western traditions: they were proud of and educated in their early days by the high culture of China but at the same time were disdainful of the corruption and fragility of China. They hated the aggression of Western powers that has pushed China to the brink of extinction but could not help embracing 'Mr. Democracy' and 'Mr. Science' with optimism and desperate hope for national salvation. Chineseness, in both culture and politics, was scorned by mainstream intellectuals. The once unified view of life and society in China was shattered. In the 1920s, poetry reflected bewilderment, including Guo Moruo's boundless self like his 'Heavenly Dog' (1920) and the over optimistic belief in the perfect future that was projected into the reality constructed by love and beauty – seen in the carefully weighted verses of Xu Zhimo and the Crescent Moon Society between the 1920s and 1930s.

The complex had resulted in the identity crisis suffered by poets like Bian in the 1930s. The relegation of anything Chinese caught Chinese intellectuals between the fragments of a glorious past and an uncertain future. 'Solitary, anxious, and nostalgic, overwhelmed by a sense of futility and desperation', they turned inward, seeking in artistic creation, a world of new coherence.[30]

THE BACKWARD-LOOKING UTOPIA: *XIANG CHOU*

In previous sections, discussions on Bian's cosmology and his search for inner peace seem to correspond to the Western nostalgic yearning for a peaceful past juxtaposed against the unsatisfactory present. However, a key anxiety driving the utopian impulse of Bian and his fellows lay in the clash between total iconoclasm and the longing for the classical Chinese ideal of beauty in denial. Therefore, nihilism is hardly the focus of any mainstream school in New Poetry. This quality – which I will refer to as '*xiang chou*' – at the same time, does not evoke key issues in the Western concept of nostalgia such as anti-urbanism, regionalism, corporatism, and doubts about the new technology in the cultural and art historical discourse. Moreover, *xiang chou* has much to do with the cultural system in ancient Chinese mythology of ancestral worship.

Consisting of two expressive Chinese characters, *xiang chou*乡愁 is a human emotion towards, first, *xiang* 乡, which means a home village. The second character, *chou* 愁, is a vivid representation of a delicate and subtle emotion experienced by generations of Chinese intellectuals. The character *chou* 愁 (sorrow) forms itself on the basis of *xin* 心 (heart), since the emotion is perceived in the heart; the upper part of is the character *qiu* 秋 (autumn), a combination of the characters *he* 禾 (crops) and *huo* 火 (fire), symbolising the spirit of agricultural communal life and connections built amongst people on the basis of traditional ethics.

Xiang chou's reflection in Chinese literature, from the classical period to modern and contemporary time, emphasizes the metaphysical solitude and the consequential collective consciousness that yearns for familiarity and intimacy, a spiritual land to return to, rather than the physical place of one's dwelling. Therefore, *xiang chou* is evoked, in most cases, during a spiritual exile. That is to say, for poets like Bian, the metaphysical solitude could not be resolved simply by staying in their home country; even more, the fact that they are not outside of China increases their *xiang chou* as they witness the internal and external existential crisis of China, both physically and spiritually.

In all cases, the ideal home constructed with *xiang chou*, acquires many features of the backward-looking utopia described by Paul Tillich:

> One of the most important insights into the essence of utopia is that every utopia creates a foundation for itself in the past – that there are backward-looking utopias just as there are forward-looking ones. In other words, which is envisioned as the ideal in the future is at the same time that which is projected as 'once upon a time in the past – or as that from which one comes and to which one seeks to return'.[31]

As Ernst Bloch wrote in *The Principle of Hope*, 'Dreams of a better life are primarily dreams that look in the first instance to the past, but then also to the future'.[32] This corresponds to the essence of *xiang chou*: it attributes honour, glory, and happiness to 'the past' while detesting 'the present'; at the same time, hope resides in 'the future', where honour, glory, and the happiness of 'the past' are restored. To a certain extent, *xiang chou*, and the backward-looking utopia, represents the Chinese understanding of the correlation of past and future. In the context of eager modernisation and passionate effort to transform the national character, *xiang chou* stitches together past and future, mending the rupture of time, which sits in the centre of classical Taoist, Confucian, and Buddhist doctrine.

I repeatedly use the term 'in search of inner peace' in analysing Bian's construction of an ideal spiritual world. It has much to do with the underlying psychology of *xiang chou*. Levenson raises the point that nationalism offers an emotional justification for Chinese intellectuals to depart from tradition. At the same, it is worth noting that, emotionally, the departure is incomplete. The construction of *xiang chou* utopia relies heavily on the emotional need of intellectuals who reluctantly broke away from their cherished tradition. Comfort is offered only by a future in which the past could be retrieved. Therefore, *xiang chou* utopia does not have much to do with the Western utopia's providing a 'screenshot' or the blueprint of a brand new future; rather, it is constructed as a daydream, which made it possible that Bian and his peers, deep in despair and disappointment with the present, to gather hope and strength in their self-imposed exile.

ANXIETY AND THE ABSENCE OF TRADITION

The utopian impulse of Chinese intellectuals shows its face in three types of anxiety in the New Poetry Movement: the anxiety of ethics, text, and culture.

The theories and practice of the early May Fourth intellectuals were mainly concerned with the function of poetry and how it could be used as a political and social instrument. Therefore, the birth of New Poetry embodies the justification of its social ethics. The anxiety of ethics is most obviously connected to the utopian impulse as it reflects the eagerness of building a new coherent centre of culture on top of total iconoclasm.

Writing as affinity to Western poetry, despite its commonness and appealing sound of modernity, is considered in this study a formal construction of a non-existent identity. Formalism serves as a reified mental formulation without careful and sustained understanding of the complex background and realities of the Western phenomenon of writing. In Bian's case, it inevitably results in a simplification and distortion of French symbolism. Eventually, both the poet and his contemporary critiques make ambiguous judgment on modernity that, as mentioned above, exist in both classical Chinese poetry and what they call 'modern feelings'. The paradox is, of course, a result of the utopian impulse in the face of anxiety.

This leads to the anxiety of text. Chinese intellectuals sought to validate their writing through textual benchmarks to establish what they believed to be modern. However, these benchmarks were adopted from the West. *Baihua* employs a lot of vernacular English and French, Bian's much celebrated poetic ideal of 'beauty of intelligence' reflects T. S. Eliot and Paul Valerie's poetics, among others. At the same time, lack of tradition plagues the mentality of Chinese intellectuals in the New Poetry Movement. Some poets like Li Jinfa and Dai Wangshu attempted to put symbolist verses into classic style poems, which results in simplification and distortion. Bian, on the other hand, inspired by the creativity and aesthetics of classical Chinese poetry, writes poems with the firm emotional structure of late Tang poetry. However, his anxiety of culture pushes him to a guilty feeling whilst the anxiety of ethics forbids him from acknowledging tradition as his true inspiration. By hiding classical Chinese poetry underneath French symbolist poetry, tradition is weakened and understanding of Western poetry distorted.

Scholars such as Cheung, Zhang, Zhao, and Bian's student Jiang Ruoshui centre their discussions on New Poetry around the topic of balance: how to find a balance between classical Chinese poetry and influence from the West. This has much to do with the anxiety of culture.[33] Bian Zhilin is highly praised for his techniques of *huagu hua'ou* 化古化欧 (adapt Europe, transform classical China). Jiang even coins the term *tongbu weiyi* 同步位移 (simultaneous relocation of progress) to measure Bian's achievement as a modern poet. By putting emphasis on 'adapt' and 'transform' (*hua* 化), this discussion seems to engage with classical Chinese poetry, while stepping forward from its formalistic construction. However, it is not unlike the totalistic Westernism in Bian's time; the standard of modernity still lies in how much has been absorbed from the West.

CONCLUSION

Looking back at the May Fourth era and the utopian perspective of the New Poetry Movement, we can see novel features and associated problems that could offer an insight into China's early efforts to modernise.

Despite the collapse of tradition in the May Fourth era, many aesthetic and intellectual elements of classical Chinese culture survived. Various Chinese intellectuals of the period still took for granted classical ideals of beauty and morality, though they often gave them new names. In Bian's case, 'the beauty of intelligence', 'crystallisation', and, most notably, 'that Western school' (French symbolist poetry) are good examples. The acceptance of Western ideology as part of a modern national identity led to an inter-textuality in New Poetry that was only formalistic. Ignoring key utopian impulses in the New Poetry Movement has hindered intellectuals' attempts to find a coherent centre for integrating into tradition new ideas and social values from the West. The utopian impulse in the Chinese society since the May Fourth era conflicts with the construction of the prescriptive system of modern Chinese philosophy. Therefore, even today, Chinese intellectuals are continuing debates on issues that define the very bases of literature, society, and modern identity – such as civilian vs aristocratic culture, nationalism vs Westernism, individualism vs collectivism, and romanticism vs modernism.

More importantly, as political discourse replaces individual discourse with a non-artistic, political system of concepts, it temporarily catches the imagination of the intelligentsia's wish for a modern identity that no longer depends on Western views. But this does not resolve any fundamental issues evoked in the May Fourth arena. A political system that ignores artistic sensitivity would not only cut off Chinese intellectuals from in-depth reflection and criticism of present conditions and the mentality of postmodern utopians in the West, but also the long tradition of finding inner peace through Taoist and Buddhist ideals. The moral level of taste in literature reflecting Confucian teachings would also be lost if all interpretation of literature must be seen in terms of advocacy and political appeal. This situation has troubled the artistic space of China for a long time and especially since the Cultural Revolution. Revolutionary movement has, in an even more powerful way than during the May Fourth era, broken down the coherent cultural centre of the Chinese self. The contradictory attractions of a modernised future and an appreciation of the quiet beauty of classical art that troubled Bian Zhilin make him an especially useful figure for understanding today's China.

NOTES

1. Bian Zhilin, *Bian Zhilin Wenji* [Collected works of Bian Zhilin] (Hefei: Anhui jiaoyu chubanshe, 2002). All translations into English from Chinese are the author's own unless stated otherwise. Bian Zhilin himself has translated a selected amount of his Chinese poems into English. Those cited in this chapter are all quoted from Bian's collected works, or Robert Payne's *Contemporary Chinese Poetry* (London: Routledge, 1947).
2. Gregory Jusdanis, *Belated Modernity and Aesthetic Culture* (Minneapolis: University of Minnesota Press, 1991).
3. Related research includes Chih-Tsing Hsia, *A History of Modern Chinese Fiction*, 3rd ed. (Bloomington: Indiana University Press, 1999); Chen Pingyuan, *Chumo Lishi yu Jinru Wusi* [Touching history and entering the May Fourth Movement] (Beijing: Beijing daxue chubanshe, 2010); Wang Zuoliang, *Wenxue Jian de Pihe* [Consonance of literatures] (Beijing: Waiyu jiaoxue yu yanjiu chubanshe, 2005); David Der-wei Wang, *Fin-de-siècle Splendor: Repressed Modernities of Late Qing Fiction, 1848–1911* (Stanford, CA: Stanford University Press, 1997); Shi Shumei, *The Lure of the Modern: Writing Modernism in Semicolonial China, 1917–1937* (Berkeley: University of California Press, 2001); Leo Ou-fan Lee, 'Literary Trends I: The Quest for Modernity, 1895–1927', in Merle Goldman and Leo Ou-fan Lee, eds., *An Intellectual History of Modern China* (Cambridge: Cambridge University Press, 2002), 142–195.
4. Ban Wang, *The Sublime Figure of History* (Stanford, CA: Stanford University Press, 1997).
5. Lee, 'Literary Trends I', 142–143.
6. Hsia, *History of Modern Chinese Fiction*, 536.
7. Xu Zhimo, 'Xinyue de Taidu' [The attitude of the Crescent Moon Society], *Xinyue* 1 (1) (1928): 4.
8. Jiang Ruoshui, *Bian Zhilin Shiyi Yanjiu* [A study of Bian Zhilin's art in poetry] (Hefei: Anhui jiaoyu chubanshe, 2005), 15; Bian Zhilin, *Bian Zhilin Wenji*, 14.
9. Harold Nicolson, *Paul Verlaine* (London: Constable & Company, 1921), 236.
10. Nicolson, *Paul Verlaine*, 239.

11. Bian Zhilin, *Bian Zhilin Wenji*, 447.
12. Qi Tang, 'Bian Zhilin yu Xiandaizhuyi Shige' [Bian Zhilin and modernist poetry], in Yuan Kejia, ed., *Bian Zhilin yu Shi Yishu* [Bian Zhilin and the art of poetry] (Shijiazhuang: Hebei jiaoyu chubanshe, 1991), 19.
13. Liang Zongdai, *Liang Zongdai Wenji* [Collected works of Liang Zongdai], vol. 2 (Beijing: Zhongyang bianyi chubanshe, 2003), 62.
14. Liang Zongdai, *Liang Zongdai Wenji*, vol. 2, 60.
15. Lloyd Haft, *Pien Chih-lin* (Dordrecht: Foris, 1983), 38.
16. T. S. Eliot, 'Tradition and the Individual Talent', *Egoist* 6 (4) (September 1919), 54.
17. Li Jianwu, *Li Jianwu Wenxue Pinglun Xuan* [Selected works of Li Jianwu's literary criticism] (Yinchuan: Ningxia renmin chubanshe, 1983), 94.
18. Li Jianwu, *Li Jianwu Wenxue Pinglun Xuan*, 118.
19. Payne, *Contemporary Chinese Poetry*, 85. This is Bian Zhilin's own translation.
20. Bian Zhilin, *Bian Zhilin Wenji*, 446.
21. Bian Zhilin, *Bian Zhilin Wenji*, 446.
22. Bian Zhilin, *Bian Zhilin Wenji*, 155.
23. Wang Guowei, *Renjian Cihua* [Commentaries on lyrical work] (Shanghai: Shanghai guji chubanshe, 1998), chap. 3.
24. Wang Guowei, *Renjian Cihua*, chap. 3.
25. Wai-Lim Yip, Diffusion of Distances: Dialogue between Chinese and Western Poetics (Berkeley: University of California Press, 1993), 202.
26. Bian Zhilin, *Bian Zhilin Wenji*, 444.
27. Nicolson, *Paul Verlaine*.
28. Bian Zhilin, *Bian Zhilin Wenji*, 459.
29. 'Tao Yuanming: Yinjiu' [Translation: 'Drinking Wine' (Tao Yuanming)], East Asia Student (blog), 6 July 2011, https://eastasiastudent.net/china/classical/tao-yuanming-drinking-wine/.
30. Yan Yu and Guo Shaoyu, *Cang Lang Shihua Jiaoshi* [Annotated *Cang Lang Shihua*] (Beijing: Renmin wenxue chubanshe, 1961), 151.
31. Paul Tillich, *Political Expectation* (New York: Harper & Row, 1971), 133.
32. Tillich, *Political Expectation*, 133.
33. Jiang Ruoshui, *Bian Zhilin Shiyi Yanjiu*.

3
The China Dream: Harmonious Dialectics and International Law

Yonit Manor-Percival

On 5 June 2019, during a state visit to Russia, Xi Jinping alluded to China (and Russia) as the states tasked with protecting an international law-based order which has come under threat. The declaration confirmed a long-standing surmise that China was looking to play a bigger part in the shaping of the inter-state space. However, in a global topography that is dominated by capitalist rationality with its myth of self-regulating, competing free markets and a reality of hegemonic power structures, the declaration also raises a question about how this bid for a role may play out. China's path to modernity and incorporation evolved for a long time outside of historical capitalism and the club of Western states which presided over its expansion. It was shaped by the experience of being semi-colonised and, for a while at least, direction was sought within the non-capitalist camp. Seen as an outsider and the 'other', the country also seems familiar. It appears to speak the language of transnational capitalism and adopt its juridical arrangements. Yet, by invoking the uniqueness of its own ways, it also presents a challenge to orthodoxies.

The world through Chinese eyes may be gleaned from the country's 'China Dream' and 'Harmonious World' paradigms. This chapter seeks to interrogate their coherence using the prism of international law (IL). The law is suitable as a prism because it occupies a central place in the country's vision of the future. It also articulates and legitimises extant logics and power structures. The chapter argues that with IL's roots in the colonial encounter and its claims to civilisational universalism it may conflict with dreams of peaceful, non-prescriptive diversity that derive from ancient – non-capitalist –

philosophy. This indicates a fault line that problematises the Chinese paradigm.

The chapter will start by looking at the historical backdrop to China's quest for modernity. It will then examine the paradigm and its dialectics, followed by commentary on IL and a concluding discussion of the faultline produced by the attempt to bring the two together. Before proceeding I would like to make clear that I do not address the role played by China's socialist heritage in the intricate tapestry that makes up the country's journey to modernity; I am focused on a different but complementary aspect. Furthermore, I am not attempting a definitive judgement but contributing to an ongoing debate. Finally, I write as an outsider, but an outsider with many years' experience of China's transformations.

INNOVATING A DREAM

In November 2012, on the occasion of his visit to the *Road to Revival* exhibition in China's National Museum, Xi Jinping, then newly appointed general secretary of the Chinese Communist Party (CCP), mapped out his vision for the country going forward. This vision was noted for its themes of national rejuvenation, moderately prosperous society, happiness, rule of law, and the path of socialism with Chinese characteristics; it came to be known as the China Dream (*Zhongguo Meng*). It became a core theme of Xi's leadership, the subject of speeches and posters, open to a spectrum of interpretations both at home and abroad.[1] Winberg Chai and May-lee Chai consider that, at least in one respect, it represented a turning point. No other leader since the establishment of the People's Republic of China (PRC), they say, had used the word 'dream' before: 'The Chinese people were told to work, to study, but never to dream.'[2] Yet Xi's address remains embedded in the ideal of collective revival and the common efforts called upon to bring it about. That the China Dream had its first airing on the occasion of Xi's visit to the *Road to Revival* exhibition thus seems apposite. Both share a preoccupation with national renewal. Such preoccupation has produced a constant flow of theory, policy, law, and state formations said to have been triggered by China's 'century of humiliation'. The term 'century of humiliation' conveys the violence of the country's forcible incorporation into the world order through being the object of European and Japanese colonial penetration. This trauma, in the manner of neoliberal 'shock therapy', was a watershed moment. When Europe's capitalist 'Great Transformation' collided with China's 'Great Divergence' it propelled the country towards its own rupture.[3] The effect was to blow apart China's ancient identity and launch the country on a quest for a robust, 'modern' one. Throughout, even in periods in which self-reliance was the guiding principle for the way forward, this continuing quest, its inflections and its adaptations remained connected with the world outside China.

The premise that the domestic and international arenas are inseparable may be traced back as far as China's tributary system, a time when 'external order was so closely related to her internal order that one could not long survive without the other'.[4] As to present days, 'China's perception of its own international role,' says Zhu Liqun, 'is driven to a great extent by outside factors'.[5] It is therefore befitting that in his speech to the 2015 Boao Forum for Asia, and again in 2018, Xi posited the China Dream as contingent on the prevalence of harmony beyond state borders. In the harmonious world, Xi elucidated, differences would not stand in the way of inclusive and peaceful cooperation. Interdependency and exchanges would coalesce with national independence, the preservation of civilisational diversity and a self-determined path to development. The principles of peaceful coexistence established by African and Asian nations in the Bandung Conference would prevail. For its part, the Chinese nation, he said, holds high its ancient philosophies: 'harmony is the most valuable', 'peace and harmony should prevail', and 'all men under heaven are brothers'.[6] With these words, Xi summoned Confucian utopianism to articulate a vision of a desired modern world order – the states of 'Great Unity' or 'Great Harmony' (*datong*) and 'Eternal Peace' (*taiping*) being the final stage of human development, now to be commingled with contemporary structures of globalised governance.[7] In so doing, Xi followed on from the Harmonious World (*hexie shijie*) narrative advanced seven years earlier by his predecessor, Hu Jintao, producing a line of continuity between the two presidencies.

In invoking the theme of a harmonious world as the framework within which to situate China's dream, Xi and Hu before him were the latest of a line of Chinese scholars and statesmen who sought to integrate the Confucian ideal into their theorisation of present realities and an envisaged future order. From the nineteenth century onwards, China's response to the dystopia visited upon it by its encounter with the West comprised a mixture of iconoclasm and nativism. Imported theories and ideologies were important protagonists in the project of new consciousness and national regeneration. Yet, indigenous conventions continued to run through social reforms either separately or in dialogue with their foreign counterparts.[8] Xiufen Lu, for example, locates on this continuum three of the country's foremost thinkers: Kang Youwei, Sun Yat-sen, and Li Dazhao.

Kang Youwei, leader of the Hundred Days Reform of the late Qing Dynasty injected the ideal of Great Harmony with Western concepts of progress, justice, equality, and constitutional monarchy. As to the world outside and China's place within it, he turned to the Confucian virtue of benevolence (*ren*) to depict a future based on communal and egalitarian principles. Though not known as a Marxist, his utopia echoes communist ideals of a classless and stateless world in which private property is no more. Sun Yat-sen, leader of the 1911 Xinhai Revolution, looked to state control over industry and land redistribution as the means by which harmony could be achieved within a system of liberal democracy. It was to be predicated on equality and secured livelihood. In this, Sun is said to have been guided by the Confucian belief that government's function is to use resources for society's benefit. Rather than the absence of poverty per se, just distribution was the prerequisite for a harmonious order. Li Dazhao's reading of Western ideas was greatly shaped by his formal education in the Chinese classics. It was this anchoring in a Confucian-type harmonious society and world, argues Lu, which predisposed China's first (if little known) Marxist and others of his generation to socialist thinking. For him, too, a harmonious world of cooperation between nations which flows from the Confucian ideal of human love, was a precondition for individual liberation. Hence, 'those who strive to be free must work hard to improve the structure of the world'.[9] Guo adds to this line of Chinese utopian thinkers Hong Xiuquan, leader of the Taiping Rebellion, who imbued the concept of eternal peace with Christian moral codes, and Mao Zedong, who embraced Marxism in pursuit of his vision of a socialist China. In present times, Xi's and Hu's 'Harmonious World paradigm' (HWP) comes on the heels of an initial concerted drive to learn from the West. They are said to have searched for a better world, or what Guo, following Lewis Munford, terms 'utopia of reconstruction'. All 'share the Confucian dream of uniting the world into a global community'.[10]

Transforming contemporary globalisation into a global community, one that lives in peace and cooperative harmony, is indeed at the heart of the HWP. Hu summed it up in eight characters: *daijiu heping, gongtong cairong*, meaning 'lasting peace and common prosperity'.[11] Countries and their people, said Hu, are bound together by a system of shared values. At its core lies the aspiration to realise their sovereign right to economic prosperity. Yet, within this overarching common interest, diverse civilisational norms and national variations will continue to operate also as a matter of right – 'the right of the peoples of each State to freely choose their social system and their path of development' without external interference.[12] The HWP upholds the virtues of and affirms China's commitment to free trade and investment, as well as economic openness and interdependency. Simultaneously, though, it also takes issue with the systemic inequality in access to the world's wealth, technology, and institutions; it posits the need for change in the way globalisation is managed and asserts the capacity of transformations to take place peacefully. From its assumed position as a leader of the camp of developing countries, China, being the biggest, calls for a Confucian 'unity without uniformity' in the collaborative endeavour of reconstituting an order of a commonly prosperous world.[13] Yet, it is to be also a rule-based order, specifically international law and its foundational concepts of equal sovereignty and non-intervention.

This pledge to adhere to the rule of law both domestically and internationally is part of the continuity of Hu's and Xi's leadership. Yet, the path leading to this point was not a straight one. It is said that the appearance of the rule of law in Chinese discourse and institutional reforms came about in response to the violent upheaval of the Cultural Revolution, in order to replace personal relationships (*ren zhi*) and political campaigns with legality (*fa zhi*) as an agent of societal progress. This not uncommon narrative seems to imply either that revolutionary China was devoid of juridical structures, or that such structures, agents of predictability and stability, were incompatible with policies that sought to raise political consciousness through mass participation. Yet, legal instruments introduced in the wake of the Xinhai Revolution persisted into the post-1949 period.[14] It was only when China embarked on its own socialist path independently of the Soviet Union that education and persuasion (including through mass movements) became the primary framework for resolving societal contradictions. Law, declared Mao in 1957, amounted to dictatorship formerly thought suitable only for barbarians, a statement that resonates with the Confucian view of law as a last resort.[15] In the Confucian harmonious world, law is to be turned to only when ethical instruction, understanding, and reconciliation – the main regulators of private and societal relations – have failed. Frequent recourse to litigation was to be a sign of civilisational degeneration. Paradoxically, it was at the height of China's revolutionary period that the country's version of modernity recuperated past traditions.

The rule of law as a concept first emerged formally in China in the 1990s. It coincided with China's growing pursuit of 'open door' policies, a development model in which foreign investment is seen as a force for advancement. For this model to work, the country had to implement that which foreign capital requires – an institutional framework capable of enforcing property rights. It was against this backdrop that the move was made to restore private property. For many of China's nineteenth- and twentieth-century thinkers and statesmen the abolition of private property was a condition necessary for the equality and justice of a harmonious world; Xi and Hu's 'people's republic' reinstated private property in both the constitution and in property legislation.

Commitment to international law in its present form followed. The words 'in its present form' are pertinent, for, in what is broadly referred to as the pre-1979 period, China was the leader of the movement for a New International Economic Order (NIEO). With regards to international law, the aspiration was to inject it with normative content that takes account of the aspirations and newly gifted sovereignty of former colonial territories who had not participated in its making. Thus, China endorsed Egypt's right to nationalise the Suez Canal, describing such a right as both legal and moral. As late as April 1974, at the Special Session of the UN Assembly, Deng Xiaoping declared China's support for developing countries' permanent sovereignty over their natural resources and their right to control and regulate all foreign investment, including the unconditional right to nationalise it. In the same year, Chinese scholars endorsed the exclusion of international law from the Charter for Economic Rights and Duties of States (CERDS). Both the inviolability of private property and the principle of state responsibility for injury to aliens were publicly renounced. International law as it is, said the late Huan Xiang, senior diplomat and chairman of the Chinese Society of International Law, 'reflected the interest and demands of the bourgeoisie, the colonialists and in particular the imperialists' and was used by them 'as a means to carry out aggression, oppression and exploitation'.[16] However, this position was not to last. The adoption of a development model based on the absorption of foreign private capital signalled integration into capitalist globalisation and its tenets of fused borders insofar as trade and foreign investment were concerned. This included membership of the World Trade Organization, a rush to conclude international investment agreements (IIAs) increasingly modelled on the Western prototype, and commitment to the United Nations that went all the way to participation in peace keeping operations. Yet echoes of the NIEO, such as the extension of the principles of sovereignty and self-determination to the economic and social arenas continue to reverberate in the HWP.

This is where matters seem to rest, at least for the moment. Material conditions and aspirations played a determinative role throughout the twists and turns of China's resolve to shed its title as the 'sick man of Asia'. Against a backdrop of national empowerment understood in terms of industrialisation, modernity, and wealth creation, it transformed mass mobilisation for liberation into enduring mobilisation for production. By now, as part of what Wang Hui termed the 'fantasy of development' and the 'myth of transition', socialism has been declared to be in its primary stage and in need of adaptation to

Chinese specificities.[17] In accordance with the principle of 'seeking truth from facts' (*shishi qiu shi*), its complete implementation is relegated to an unspecified future time – it remains an ideal.

Also, by now Xi presides over a state that is ever more incorporated into capitalist globalisation and, with deepening reforms, is increasingly responsive to foreign capital's needs. China's classification during Hu's presidency as a member of the camp of developing countries has been thrown into question by breakneck economic growth. Albeit not exclusively, China's assumed role as the developing countries' leader is centred around the promotion of trade and investment, with its pinnacle, the Belt and Road Initiative.[18] At the institutional level, commitment to the rule of law is actualised through a host of IIAs and legislative reforms promulgated after study of Western practices. The Foreign Investment Law which came into effect on 1 January 2020 guarantees foreign investors greater freedom of entry and establishment, a say in the formulation of regulations, and reduced supervision. Peaceful coexistence notwithstanding, the Chinese army is being nurtured into becoming a world-class force. From the imperial perspective of the US, China's technological innovations and 'going global' (*zou chuqu*) ambitions have upgraded it from an anticipated threat to a perceived real and present one. Catching up with the West – always central to CCP debates about the way forward – is finally within grasp.

Within this intricate tapestry of innovative ideas and practices, the WHP may be described as a vision of partial incorporation, one not subservient to prescribed sameness. The proposition seems to be that first, changes may be effected through what is described from Western perspective as shallow integration – that is, being both 'in and out', simultaneously an insider and the other, promoting interstate cooperation whilst engaging in globalised market-based competition. Second, it is proposed that the parameters of incorporation may be controlled peacefully, notably through compliance with legal rules. Yet, globalisation and international law form part of a single eco-political-juridical ensemble, in which, as pointed out by Hannah Arendt, capitalist never-ending accumulation of property necessitates structures that facilitate the never-ending accumulation of power.[19] Impulses for prescriptive, and all too often coercive, conflictual, and violent expansion find expression in legal structures that are legitimised by a narrative of universalism. Viewed through the lens of Chinese philosophy, such universalism negates the existence of the 'other' and is therefore out of step with the oneness of 'all under heaven' (*tianxia*). This includes the Confucian virtue of reciprocity – the heart-to-heart felt respect extended to others. Universalism, says Zhao Tingyang, one of China's leading philosophers, is 'a sort of fundamentalism that insists on the ideology of making others a pagan'.[20] As shall be seen below, the existence of conflicts in a harmonious world is not disregarded. Yet, they are understood as relative and lacking in ontological finality. The transition from difference to conflict may be avoided through interaction within a framework of human moral cultivation. Given the fundamental nature of these contradictions, the question arises as to whether this state of being both 'in and out' can be maintained, and, if so, whether this can be done peacefully. To explore this question further it is necessary to go into the interior of both discourses, starting with the notion of a harmonious world.

HARMONIOUS DIALECTICS – UNITY AND DIVERSITY

The HWP's preoccupation is with the historically well-rehearsed issues of development and peace. However, it is neither a Kantian prescription for the establishment of peace, nor is it Fukuyama's end point of history. Rather, it articulates China's understanding of where we are now and what we may potentially achieve by acting in harmony with existing dispositions in the international arena. Importantly for present purposes, where we are now is not a reflection of a universalist law of nature but the product of a triad of present conditions, the strategy that these conditions call for, and the end result of its successful implementation. Where we are now is product of 'the international balance of power' that is currently changing 'in favour of the maintenance of world peace', but the immanent dynamic of which may lead to a different disposition.[21] What we may potentially achieve is driven by a desire for peace that is inseparable from the right to subsistence, stated as early as 1991 to be the primary human right from which all other rights derive.[22] In other words, 'peace and development' is posited as the current condition, a choice between well-being and perishing, and the object of the global undertaking. Peace is both a prerequisite for and the outcome of development moving to a stage of common prosperity.[23]

This triad articulates the three core concepts which make up what Qin Yaqin terms Chinese 'harmonious dialectics'.[24] Understanding these concepts, he argues, is pivotal to grasping the logic of the HWP. The first is harmony (*he*). Here the premise is that 'any two opposites in a process are fundamentally non-conflicting and contradictions can be solved through complementary interaction before a new synthesis is born'.[25] The second is situational dispositions (*shi*), which Zhu Liqun posits as central to understanding China's relationship with the outside world.[26] *Shi* refers to a 'disposition' that permanently sways between the static and the dynamic, but the movement of which has little in common with aspirations for a final truth, for its perpetual movement is immanent.[27] Thus, 'the only proposition that does not change is that everything else is subject to change'.[28] There is a transformative spontaneity – the unavoidable movement that is independent of external intervention, yet calls for corresponding action. The third key concept is becoming (*bian*). Here, actors and institutions transform and are transformed as part of their interactive identity formation and in line with situational dispositions. Central to becoming is the interdependent and complementary relationship between differences. Essential properties are not self-standing but are determined by interactive energy that is forever in process. This reconciliatory, non-zero gaming process in which each includes, complements, and absorbs the other is the essence of a harmonic whole. From the interconnectedness of complementary differences harmony arises to form unity without uniformity.[29] Thus, in the process of harmonisation, change is a life-enhancing, creative moment. Conflict and antagonism may be resolved or avoided through human moral cultivation and adjustment to nature, and 'all differences and conflicts among things have no ontological ultimacy'.[30] Such a process, argues Qin, is essentially different from the Hegelian-Marxist concept: while in Chinese dialectics A is inclusive of non-A, so that one evolves into the other, in Hegelian dialectics,

A and B represent separate, determinate, and independent entities. Their confrontation can be resolved only through domination or annihilation. Thus, rather than being an essential part of the process of harmonisation, conflict represents an unavoidable and unresolvable moment of objective truth by means of which reality progresses along a linear, idealistic (whether spiritual or material) line.[31]

In China's understanding of contemporary international dispositions, the pursuit of peace, development, and cooperation is the 'irresistible trend of the times'.[32] There is also an 'irreversible' progress toward a multipolar world.[33] The residual threat to peace and development originates from the operation of hegemonic politics and the ever-widening global north–south gap they create.[34] Globalisation is a 'double-edged sword'.[35] On the one hand, development opportunities are opened up by a technologically innovative, integrated, and internationalised system of production. On the other hand, developing countries are increasingly impoverished, marginalised, and subjugated because this same globally integrated production system is under the hegemonic control of developed countries and their multinationals. The potential of globalisation as a peace-enhancing endeavour is hindered by the residues of imperialist rule that once inflicted such great suffering on the Chinese people. Consequently, developing economies find themselves in a subordinate position – the survival of their economies is put into the hands of others.[36]

In sum, the harmonious world is one of fluidity, flexibility, multiplicity, multipolarity, the reciprocity of 'win-win' cooperation, and the resolution of conflict through interaction and cultivated understanding. In the words of *People's Daily*: 'The multipolarisation of the world is a reflection of the diversity of the world. The world is colorful and varied in posture, and the mode of development is diversified. There should not and cannot be such a phenomenon that when "my flowers blossom, a hundred other flowers will wither away"'.[37] Chinese understanding is that peace and development are contingent on – in Confucian terms – the oneness of all under heaven showing itself in diversity. The unfolding is guided by 'the general will of the people' (*min xin*) – their autonomy to follow or not to follow.[38]

INTERNATIONAL LAW – WORLD ORDER BY DESIGN

IL is said to be 'the critical institution of an international society and the mark that relations among states embody shared rules and norms'.[39] This statement articulates the idea that IL derives from a system of norms distilled into rules. Having morphed into an institution, these norms and rules prescribe and lock in the formal and informal principles of international conduct and practice, foreclosing alternatives and underlaying the exercise of power.

Power may take on different forms. It may be direct and overt, as in the case of the use of military force, or it may be indirect and covert, as when it is exercised for the design and production of subjectivities and institutions.[40] Michael Doyle singled out design as a hallmark of an empire. An edifice of control is constructed, so that the imperial actor can achieve outcomes the subordinate one may not desire.[41] In the context of globalisation, which Wood terms the 'empire of capital', the aim is to bring countries within the grasp of US-designed institutional architecture. Their sovereignty, formal equality, absoluteness, and immunity from intervention is in practice to be exercised in a manner that facilitates the transformation of variegated communities into uniform market societies.

The idea that the informal and impersonal operation of so-called free markets is in reality predicated on preordained design seems at first blush counterintuitive. Yet, as observed by Polanyi, laissez-faire was 'not a method to achieve a thing; it was the thing to be achieved'. Rather than an instance of 'spontaneous progress', laissez-faire was planned. In the historical process of 'double movement' – that of the 'disembedding' of the economy from society on the one hand and its contestation on the other – it is only the latter that is not premeditated.[42] In the context of capitalist globalisation, with multinational networks acting as interconnected arteries through which globalised capital passes, the capacity to ensure uniform compliance is essential if blockages are to be avoided. Capital's compulsion to migrate speedily from one place of poverty to another and to link them with centres of wealth requires not only freedom of movement, but a say in the way sovereignty is exercised upon territorial penetration. Capital is assisted in this by a blueprint drawn up by a cohort of core states, international financial institutions, elite policy-planning organisations, think tanks, and corporate lobbying groups. Such a blueprint includes the design of IL (the international legal regime of international investment law) which prioritises private property rights over public interest and gives foreign investors a judicial category of greater protection.

The normative content of IL's institutional design may be gleaned from Article 38(1)(c) of the Statute of International Law, 1945. It counts among its sources 'general principles of law recognized by civilized nations'. The provision reflects classical IL, in which the equality was attendant on admission into the family of nations, which admission was itself contingent on meeting a standard of civilisation. The legal criterion comprised principles of civility – that is, the protection the state extended to life, liberty, and the property of foreigners, and the extent to which such protection was congruent with the requirements of a rule of law as designed by European countries. On the one hand, admission pointed to interconnectedness and interdependency between European and non-European nations; on the other, such interconnectedness played out in a balance of power weighted in favour of Europe. It entitled the Europeans to design and recast non-Western societies in their own image and in a manner that supported their commercial ambitions. Thus, the distillation of norms and rules of IL developed hand in hand with overseas expansion. It was underpinned by a 'civil–savage' dichotomy whereby European statehood was deemed uniquely civilised, entitling its members to draft the rules of admission.

The dynamics of connectivity and control may be found in early European writings, such as the sixteenth-century jurist and theologian Francisco de Vitoria. His 1539 addresses ('*Relectio de Indis*') are regarded as founding texts of IL. They influenced Grotius, the main progenitor of IL. Vitoria sought to explain the colonial encounter between the Spaniards and the 'Indians' by replacing divine law with a theory of natural law in which the 'Indians' emerged as ontologically equal by virtue of their human capacity to access reason and rationality. They possessed 'true dominion, both in private and public affairs'.[43] Yet, their ontological equality was undermined by customs that did not measure up to universal norms. Thus, the 'Indian' human potential was to be realised under Spanish tutelage. In the event of 'Indian' contestations, this arrangement of 'natural partnership and communication' was to be protected by a right to a 'just war'.[44] By the nineteenth century, James Lorimer divided humanity into three categories: first, civilised, Western, state-organised societies with their commitment to the rule of law and the protection of personal liberties; second, 'barbarous' humanity who developed state formations the governance of which nevertheless fell short of European standards; third, 'savage' humanity comprising simple people who lacked any semblance of organised rule. That the benchmark for this taxonomy was the degree and quality of statist organisation reflected the fact that by that time, in Europe, international law had moved on to positivism.[45] Yet, natural law continued to be applied to non-Europeans to underscore their inferiority. Lorimer grounded in it the inequality among states. Thus, 'savage' people were entitled only to humane treatment whereas the partially civilised qualified for partial recognition. Members of the first category had the right to dominate those of the second and colonise those of the third. [46]

Both the view of IL as the product of an exclusive club of European states and the assertion that their civilisational rules were imposed on others are subject to scholarly debate. The proposition that colonialism was central to IL's formation is stated to be incomplete, eurocentric, and in need of replacement with an 'intercivilizational perspective'.[47] The colonial encounter, it is argued, was not the cradle of IL. Rather, it was a moment of capture, a time when European positivist jurisprudence unilaterally appropriated and thereby destroyed a preceding, pluralistic, and more inclusive juridical order. Under that order, independent legal systems known to the Europeans and acknowledged by them as equal formed a universal consensus that linked people all over the world. On this view, decolonialisation ended a brief yet distorting interlude in the history of IL. For Antony Anghie, by contrast, the dissemination of sovereignty to formerly colonised territories was a time when (at least when seen through a European lens) the IL they had created reached its truly universalist apex. Doctrines such as state succession and acquired rights supported the proposition that, having assumed statehood, the new states were deemed to have accepted the IL that went with it, ensuring there was to be no demarcation line between colonialism and its aftermath.[48] Seen from this perspective, IIAs and the challenge they pose to sovereignty in general and economic sovereignty in particular are integral to these efforts to preserve an imperialist status quo, even if informally.

As to IL's modality of expansion, Arnold Becker Lorca for example moves away from the prevailing narratives of admission and imposition to suggest a different route. That is, the voluntary appropriation of European IL by non-European lawyers who came to the continent during the second half of the nineteenth century. Not only did these lawyers accept the standard of civilisation as a minimum requirement for joining the family of nations, they also agreed that European law was the measure of such standard. Yet, and of particular interest for present purposes, whilst internalising European principles, non-European jurists also adapted them to, or at least contextualised them by reference to, their own national needs, cultural heritages, and the specificities of their legal regimes. By the end of the century, this dual process of internalisation and indigenisation produced the occasional challenge to the standard of civilisation, as when, for example, it was described as unscientific and deceitful. On this view, European IL was universalised by means of interaction and transnational conversations which rendered it simultaneously pluralistic and universal.[49]

The probability is that both imposition and appropriation were in operation at different times and places. In any event, the gulf between the two is much reduced once the other limb of imperial interconnectivity is introduced. That is, design, control, and power, including their discursive and subjectivity-producing manifestations. It was the non-Europeans who felt compelled to adjust themselves to the rules of European modernity rather than the other way round – but that had not always been the case. King Henry VIII sent a mission to Turkey to study Suleiman II's legal code. Sixteenth-century jurists and philosophers praised Ottoman military discipline and administrative competence. Leading European enlightenment thinkers looked to China for moral instruction and guidance in institutional development. Gunpowder, printing, and the compass, three inventions which, according to Francis Bacon, changed the world, came from China. The escapement mechanism pivotal to all clockwork originated in Byzantium.[50] The direction of this flow was reversed when Europe, awash with money accumulated through conquest, slavery, and silver and gold extraction, climbed 'up the Asian shoulders' and used commodities, gunboats, and the discourse of civilisational superiority to rise from the periphery of the world to its centre.[51]

IL continues to reflect its regional origins. Beyond disagreements about processes, and IL's claim of universality, the assertion that it embodies a Western version of rationalist, liberal, and statist modernity is indisputable. IL forecloses diversity and subsumes differences, or at least holds them 'irrelevant to juridical analysis'.[52] IL, as the product of interstate hierarchical dynamics, does not lend itself easily to what Chen Xiaomei terms Occidentalism – the phenomenon whereby, once imported, external norms provoke modifications and adaptations so as to produce a new localism.[53]

The combination of connectivity and control exercised through hierarchies of power remains a major feature of the contemporary global landscape. In what Chandler calls 'empire in denial', imperial designs persist below the surface.[54] They continue to animate the way sovereignty is practiced. Positivism notwithstanding, for Friedrich Hayek, a founding father of the neoliberalism movement, the rule of law remains bound with Hume's three principles of nature: stability of possession, transfer by consent, and the performance of promises.[55] Vitoria's reasoning reverberates in the language, premise, and substantive provisions of modern IIAs.

CONCLUSION: SAME BED, DIFFERENT DREAMS

In one of his HWP addresses, Hu Jintao invoked the story of Zheng He, China's fifteenth-century admiral whose seven maritime expeditions made him the first to reach corners of the world later to be hailed as European discoveries. Yet neither Zheng He nor the imperial court pursued conquest. The mariner returned home and the expeditions came to an end. However, it was different for Zheng's Western counterparts. The 'Doctrine of Discovery', one of IL's first principles, meant that upon arrival they could lay claim to the so-called new territories. It conferred on the home country and its settlers sovereign and property rights that required no local consent. The doctrine remains part of IL to these days and continues to play a role in the management of the relationship with native people and nations.[56] Hu used the tale of Zheng He to convey China's civilisational attributes and its different vision of globalised interactions. Yet, the IL which is supposed to regulate such interactions remains bound up with expansion and conquest. Similarly, it is able to put issues on a universal plain, a hallmark of domination and hegemony. [57] China, which was forcibly integrated into the world order under IL, has now incorporated itself voluntarily into many of the norms and power structures that retain their imperialist character. They are the same norms and power structures which the HWP seeks to negate.

Arrighi analyses the reason why Zheng He's voyages did not lead to conquest by reference to the absence of capitalist logic. For non-capitalist imperial China self-reinforcement was to be found not in territorial enlargement but in the building of an integrated national economy capable of functioning as a political centre to its vassal states on whose allegiance and incorporation stability depended. Once military campaigns achieved the objectives of securing and pacifying borders, by the 1760s territorial expansion ceased.[58] Capitalist logic, by contrast, is driven by the pursuit of endless accumulation. From this flows not only the endless accumulation of power but also a compulsion for limitless territorial expansion so as to maintain or restore the rate of profit. Further, the controlled territory must be prized open and transformed so as to prevent impediments to the flow of capital. Thus, capitalism may be described as a system of frontiers and peripheries that are for ever in a state of motion and advancement. Each completed conquest signals the birth of a new one, and, with it, a new round of transformation. To this end, by a variety of means – military conquests, structural adjustments, economic warfare, sanctions, hegemonic discourse – consent is constructed; alternatively, coercion is applied. Thus, one by one divergent sovereignties and developmental paths are truncated and uniformity takes hold. This includes the Chinese socialist frontier. Whether or not China is now going down the capitalist path is a matter for debate. However, even if harmonious dialectics is to be applied (i.e, recognising that socialism and capitalism both incorporate elements of each so that they mutually re-form), capitalism's existential need for expansion and growth means that conflict rather than harmony is its natural habitat. As pointed out by Beverly Silver and Lu Zhang, 'where capital goes conflict follows'; and, as stated by Wallerstein, 'it would be a very curious reading of historical capitalism that suggested that the outcome has been harmony'.[59]

China's vision of globalised, equal, and cooperative interactions brings to mind the Confucian obligation to foster welfare, the virtue of reciprocity, and the discouragement of competition as a source of disarray by which the stability of its non-capitalist empire was underpinned. By contrast, the institutions which regulate the empire of capital, including that of IL, reflect an altogether different rationality. Insofar as capital is concerned, borders are barriers to be removed so as to facilitate its free movement, national markets are fused through technological advances, economic sovereignty is constrained and disciplined, and interests interlock. In other respects, borders remain sites of conflict, ever more secured against the free movement of people and the threat of diversity which their arrival signals. National interests compete and collide under the supervision of a hegemon with self-proclaimed entitlement to the exercise of extraterritorial jurisdiction in the pursuit of domination, regimentation, and uniformity. Technological advances and the knowledge economy create zones of both people's and states' exclusion. Veils of separation and itemisation at both the national and individual level obscure the oneness of 'all under heaven'. Suffice it to observe the US pivot to Asia, trade war with China, and the PRC's own military build-up to conclude that this type of globalisation does not lend itself to different management, at least, not peacefully. It seems that rather than representing new trends, the *shi* remains bound with the tension attendant on the disruption to the balance between the US hegemon and its perceived competitors, as well as the colonialist and imperialist impulses which gave birth to IL as we know it.

The IIAs program in which the PRC is an active participant is a case in point. China, say Wang Zonglai and Hu Bin, 'opposes any restrictions on State sovereignty that are non-reciprocal, non-voluntary and based on power politics'.[60] Yet, IIAs restrict sovereignty by constraining the state's regulatory space. Reciprocity is rendered illusory by the fact that the majority of IIAs involve one home and one host state. Mostly, treaty obligations are imposed only on the latter. Multinationals are their shadowy beneficiary – which, on the whole, are free of obligations altogether. If the HWP underscores the importance of localised solutions, IIAs operate to internationalise and homogenise them. The HWP attributes the strife that besieges the global space and the growing global north–south gap to the operation of hegemonic powers. Yet, China's integration into the IIAs program signalled her incorporation into and acceptance of a 'particularly American conception of investment rights'.[61] Seen through this lens of empire, contemporary investment treaties may be said to share the attributes of unequal colonial treaties. Like them, they serve expansive economic compulsions. A reality of power deficit is masked by a legal understanding of consent that is narrowed down to the act of signature.

To conclude, finding fault lines within the imaginings of a different order is hardly exceptional. Such imaginings address the future, yet they remain anchored in their own time. Contradictions are thus only to be expected. Thomas More's *Utopia* envisioned a society in which classes and human arrogance are eliminated through the eradication of private property. Yet, it also retains the justification that served English colonialism so well: the principle that people may be deprived of their land if they have not put it to productive use. Population growth on the island necessitated the establishment of colonies among so-called primitive people who had much uncultivated and unoccupied land. War in response to refusal to adopt the utopian way of life was justified 'when a people which does not use its soil but keeps it idle and waste nevertheless forbids the use and possession of it to others who by rule of nature ought to be maintained by it'.[62]

China's paradigm has shed its revolutionary character. In a bid to formulate a unique model of modernity, the country's heritage of Confucian rationality moved to centre stage. It seeks to bypass the confrontation between capitalism and socialism, raising the possibility of a non-Westernised path. It is too early to tell whether the fault line that runs through it renders it fatally flawed. As Mao pointed out in his treatise on contradiction, 'between the opposites in a contradiction there is at once unity and struggle, and it is this that impels things to move and change'.[63] Contradictions may cast doubt over the ease of implementation. Yet, rather than invite dismissal, they should spur us to take off our universalist lenses to see better where solutions may lie.

NOTES

1. See, for example, 'General Secretary Xi Jinping Explicates the "Chinese Dream"', *Chinese Law & Government* 48 (6) (2016): 477–479; Xi Jinping, 'Full text of Xi Jinping's report at 19th CPC National Congress', *China Daily*, 4 November 2017, http://www.chinadaily.com.cn/china/19thcpc nationalcongress/2017-11/04/content_34115212.htm; Xi Jinping, 'Full text: Keynote speech by President Xi Jinping at Opening Ceremony of 1st China International Import Expo', *Xinhua*, 5 November 2018, http://www.xinhuanet.com/english/2018-11/05/c_137583815.htm.
2. Winberg Chai and May-lee Chai, 'The Meaning of Xi Jinping's Chinese Dream', *American Journal of Chinese Studies* 20 (2) (2013): 96, 97.
3. On 'shock therapy' see Naomi Klein, *The Shock Doctrine: The Rise of Disaster Capitalism* (London: Allen Lane, 2007), 25–38. The 'Great Transformation is characterised by economic "disembedding" – society's detachment from economic imperatives and its subordination to purportedly self-regulating markets'; Karl Polanyi, *The Great Transformation: The Political and Economic Origins of Our Time* (New York: Beacon Press, 1957). On China's 'Great Divergence' see Giovanni Arrighi, *Adam Smith in Beijing: Lineages of the Twenty-First Century* (London: Verso, 2007).
4. Wang Gungwu and Zheng Yongnian, 'Introduction', in Wang Gungwu and Zheng Yongnian, eds., *China and the New International Order* (London: Routledge, 2008), 4–5.
5. Zhu Liqun, 'China's Foreign Policy Debates', Chaillot Papers, no. 121 (European Union Institute for Security Studies, 2010), 39, https://www.iss.europa.eu/sites/default/files/EUISSFiles/cp121-China_s_Foreign_Policy_Debates_0.pdf.
6. Ministry of Foreign Affairs of the People's Republic of China, 'Full Text of Chinese President's Speech at Boao Forum for China', 28 March 2015, https://www.fmprc.gov.cn/mfa_eng/wjdt_665385/zyjh_665391/t1250690.shtml. See also 'Xi Calls for Building World of Great Harmony', *Xinhua*, 11 April 2018, http://www.xinhuanet.com/english/2018-04/11/c_137103763.htm.

7. Baogang Guo, 'Utopia of Reconstruction: Chinese Utopianism from Hong Xiuquan to Mao Zedong', *Journal of Comparative Asian Development* 2 (2) (2003): 197.
8. Maurice Meisner, *Mao's China and After: A History of the People's Republic of China*, 3rd ed. (New York: Free Press, 1977) 3, 4, 14, 17–19; Timothy Brook, 'Capitalism and the Writing of Modern History in China', in Gregory Blue and Timothy Brook, eds., *China and Historical Capitalism: Genealogies of Sinological Knowledge* (Cambridge, Cambridge University Press, 1999), 128–129; Peter Moody, *Conservative Thought in Contemporary China* (Lanham, MD: Lexington Books, 2007), 21.
9. Xiufen Lu, 'The Confucian Ideal of Great Harmony (*Datong*), the Daosit Account of Change, and the Theory of Socialism in the Work of Li Dazhao', *Asian Philosophy* 21 (2) (2011): 171.
10. Guo, 'Utopia of Reconstruction', 179, 209.
11. Jean-Marc F. Blanchard and Sujian Guo, '"Harmonious World" and China's New Foreign Policy', in Sujian Guo and Jean-Marc F. Blanchard, eds. *"Harmonious World" and China's New Foreign Policy* (Lanham, MD: Lexington Books, 2008), 3.
12. Information Office of the State Council, 'White Paper: China's Foreign Policies for Pursuing Peaceful Development', September 2011, http://english.www.gov.cn/archive/white_paper/2014/09/09/content_281474986284646.htm; Hu Jintao, 'Hold High the Great Banner of Socialism with Chinese Characteristics and Strive for New Victories in Building a Moderately Prosperous Society', Report to the 17th National Congress of the Communist Party of China, 15 October 2007, http://ls.china-embassy.org/eng/zt/1ncoc/t997655.htm.
13. Information Office of the State Council, 'White Paper: China's Foreign Policies for Pursuing Peaceful Development'; 'Working Together to Build a Harmonious World is Socialist China's World Outlook', *People's Daily*, 1 December 2011.
14. Rene David and John E. C. Brierley, *Major Legal Systems in the World Today*, 3rd ed. (London: Stevens and Sons, 1985) 523, 525–526.
15. David and Brierley, *Major Legal Systems*, 528–529.
16. Kong Qingjiang, 'Bilateral Investment Treaties: The Chinese Approach and Practice', in B. S. Chimni et al., eds., *Asian Book of International Law, 1998–1999* (Leiden: Martinus Nijhoff Publishers, 2003), 108.
17. Wang Hui, *China's New Order: Society, Politics, and Economy in Transition* (Cambridge, MA: Harvard University Press, 2003) 43, 104.
18. China exercises its vote in the Security Council to resist intervention in Global South countries as, for example, in the case of Venezuela,

to whom it also provides humanitarian aid to alleviate the effects of US sanctions; 'China Delivers 71 Tons of Medical Aid to Venezuela', Venezuelanalysis.com, 15 May 2019, https://venezuelanalysis.com/news/14490.

19. Hannah Arendt, *Imperialism: Part Two of the Origins of Totalitarianism* (New York: Harvest/HBJ, 1968), 23.
20. Tingyan Zhao, 'Rethinking Empire from a Chinese Concept "All-under-Heaven" (Tian-xia)', *Social Identities* 12 (1) (2006): 37.
21. Hu Jintao, 'Hold High the Great Banner of Socialism'; Hu though goes on to say, however, that although international disposition might change 'the Chinese government and people will always pursue common development, cooperation and a peaceful, independent foreign policy'.
22. Information Office of the State Council, 'White Paper: Human Rights in China: Part 1, The Right to Subsistence – the Foremost Human Right the Chinese People Long Fight for', 1991, http://www.china.org.cn/e-white/7/index.htm.
23. Information Office, 'White Paper: China's Foreign Policies for Pursuing Peaceful Development: Part 4, China's Path to Peaceful Development is a Choice Necessitated by History'; Su Hao, 'Harmonious World: The Conceived International Order in Framework of China's Foreign Affairs' in Masafumi Iida, ed., *China's Shift: Global Strategy of the Rising Power*, National Institute for Defence Studies Joint Research Series, no. 3 (Tokyo: National Institute for Defense Studies, 2009), 31, http://www.nids.mod.go.jp/english/publication/joint_research/series3/pdf/3-2.pdf.
24. Qin Yaqing, 'International Society as a Process: Institution, Identities, and China's Peaceful Rise', *The Chinese Journal of International Politics* 3 (2) (2010): 129.
25. Qin, 'International Society as a Process', 144.
26. Zhu, 'China's Foreign Policy Debates', 17–18.
27. Francois Julien, *The Propensity of Things: Towards a History of Efficacy in China* (New York: Zone Books, 1995) 11, 17–18. The term that comes close to 'truth' in Confucian thoughts is the Way (*dao*). It denotes the sum total of truths about the universe and man; D. C. Lau, 'Introduction', in Confucius, *The Analects* (London: Penguin, 1979) 11, 13.
28. John Blofeld, trans., *The Book of Change: A New Translation of the Ancient Chinese I Ching* (Crows Nest: Allen and Unwin, 1965); Zhu, 'China's Foreign Policy Debates', 17–18; Wang Gungwu, 'China and the International Order: Some Historical Perspectives', in Wang Gungwu and Zheng Yongnian, eds., *China and the New International Order* (London: Routledge, 2008), 23.

29. Qin, 'International Society as a Process', 131, 133, 138, 144, 149.
30. Chung-Ying Cheng, 'Towards Constructing a Dialectics of Harmonization: Harmony and Conflict in Chinese Philosophy', *Journal of Chinese Philosophy* 33 (1) (2006): 25.
31. Cheng, 'Towards Constructing a Dialectics'.
32. Hu Jintao, 'Hold High the Great Banner of Socialism'; Information Office of the State Council, 'White Paper: China's Foreign Policies for Pursuing Peaceful Development'.
33. Hu Jintao, 'Hold High the Great Banner of Socialism'.
34. Hu Jintao, 'Hold High the Great Banner of Socialism'.
35. Yong Deng and Thomas G. Moore, 'China Views Globalization: Towards a New Great-Power Politics?', *Washington Quarterly* 117 (2004): 118–121.
36. Jenny Clegg, *China's Global Strategy: Towards a Multipolar World* (London: Pluto Press, 2009), 84–85.
37. 'The Falsehood of Monopolar Theory', *People's Daily*, 30 July 2003.
38. Zhao, 'Rethinking Empire', 29, 30.
39. Simon Bromley, 'Universalism and Difference in International Society', in William Brown, Simon Bromley, and Suma Athreye, eds., *A World of Whose Making? Ordering the International: History, Change and Transformation* (London: Pluto Press, 2004), 77.
40. For a taxonomy of power see, for example, Michael Barnett and Raymond Duvall, 'Power in Global Governance', in Michael Barnett and Raymond Duvall, eds., *Power in Global Governance* (Cambridge: Cambridge University Press, 2008), 1–32.
41. Michael W. Doyle, *Empires* (Cornell: Cornell University Press, 1986), 34, 37.
42. Polanyi, *The Great Transformation*, xxvii, 37, 145.
43. Anthony Pagden and Jeremy Lawrence, eds., *Vitoria: Political Writing* (Cambridge: Cambridge University Press, 2010), 251.
44. Pagden and Lawrence, *Vitoria*, 278; Antony Anghie, *Imperialism, Sovereignty and the Making of International Law* (Cambridge: Cambridge University Press, 2005), 13–23.
45. Broadly, positivism refers to the principle that laws derive their validity from the fact that they were enacted by a legitimate authority (rather than moral considerations).
46. James Lorimer, *The Institute of the Law of Nations* (William Blackwood and Sons, 1883). For a discussion of the standard of civilisation see, for example, Andrew Linklater, 'The Standard of Civilisation in World Politics', *Human Figurations* 5 (20) (2016): n.p., https://quod.lib.

umich.edu/h/humfig/11217607.0005.205/--standard-of-civilisation-in-world-politics; Gustavo Gozzi, 'The Particularistic Universalism of International Law in the 19th Century', *Harvard International Law Journal* 52 (2010): 73.

47. Yasuaki Onuma, 'When Was the Law of International Society Born?', *Journal of the History of International Law* 2 (1) (2000): 7.
48. Broadly, these doctrines refer to the principle of the continuity of obligations whereby a government is bound by rights granted to private parties by its predecessors; it encompasses the civil and international principle of *pacta sunt servanda* – agreements must be kept.
49. Arnulf Becker Lorca, 'Universal International Law: Nineteenth Century Histories of Imposition, Appropriation and Circulation', *Harvard International Law Journal* 51 (2010): 475.
50. Hugh Trevor-Roper, *The Rise of Christian Europe* (London: Thames and Hudson, 1966), 23–24.
51. Andrew Gunder Frank, *ReOrient: Global Economy in the Asian Age* (Berkeley: University of California Press, 1998), 277–283.
52. Emmanuel Jouannet, 'Universalism of International law and Imperialism: The True-False Paradox of International Law?', *European Journal of International Law* 18 (2007): 379.
53. Xiaomei Chen, *Occidentalism: A Theory of Counter-Discourse in Post-Mao China*, 2nd ed. (London: Rowman and Littlefield, 2002), 2.
54. David Chandler, *Empire in Denial: The Politics of State-Building* (London: Pluto Press, 2006).
55. F. A. Hayek, *The Constitution of Liberty* (London: Routledge, 2006), 138.
56. In 'Johnson v M'Intosh' (1823) 21 US 543, the US Supreme Court held that the Doctrine of Discovery was an established legal principle of American and European colonial law and was also federal and state law.
57. Giovanni Arrighi, *The Long Twentieth Century: Money, Power and the Origins of Our Times* (London: Verso, 2010), 29.
58. Giovanni Arrighi, 'China's Market Economy in the Long Run', in Ho-fung Hung, ed., *China and the Transformation of Global Capitalism* (Baltimore, MD: Johns Hopkins University Press, 2009), 25, 27.
59. Beverly J. Silver and Lu Zhang, 'China as an Emerging Epicenter of World Labour Unrest', in Hung, *China and the Transformation*, 177; Immanuel Wallerstein, *Historical Capitalism* (London: Verso, 1983), 34, 109.
60. Wang Zonglai and Hu Bin, 'China's Reform and Opening-Up and International Law', *Chinese Journal of International Law* 139 (2010): 197.

61. James Petras and Henry Veltmeyer, *Multinationals on Trial: Foreign Investment Matters* (Farnham: Ashgate, 2007), 111.
62. Thomas More, *Utopia* (New Haven: Yale University Press, 1965), 137.
63. Mao Zedong, 'On the Correct Handling of Contradictions among the People', http://www.marxists.org/reference/archive/mao/selected-works/volume-5/mswv5_58.htm.

4

Nostalgic Utopia in Chinese Aesthetic Modernity: The Case of the Film *Fang Hua* (Youth)

Jie Wang

Modern Chinese Aesthetics can be traced back to 1915. In that year Li Shutong 李叔同 created the famous 'Farewell Song' (*Song Bie* 送别)[1] and called into question aspects of modernism. It was also the year in which *New Youth* was first published, a periodical fundamental to the founding of the May Fourth Movement, that introduced much modern Western thought, including Darwinism, anarchism, Marxism, and utilitarianism, as well as presenting literary works in the modern spirit by authors such as Lu Xun and Zhou Zuoren. *New Youth* served as an important platform for the ideology of the 1919 May Fourth Movement.

China's modern literature and art took shape and developed a new aesthetic style symbolised by Li Shutong's 'Farewell Song', which I will call 'nostalgic utopia'. This is a trope of classical Chinese culture – the yearning for the ancestral home bound by blood ties – which was turned into a utopian mode for a new aesthetic style. It became a fundamental aesthetic form in the May Fourth Movement and continues in contemporary Chinese films and art. China had not anticipated the crushing defeat it suffered in the Sino-Japanese naval war of 1895. It had a cultural tradition of spectacular brilliance but the society was still industrially underdeveloped. In the shock of defeat and the post-war uncertainty a serious fracture of national consciousness was experienced, from which arose an intensely tragic emotional structure – nostalgic utopia. Nostalgic utopia was used as a framework for showing the process of Chinese society undergoing modernisation, a process filled with the emotion of real-life tragedy. This can be seen in works of the period such as 'Farewell Song' and Lu Xun's 'My Old Home' (*Guxiang* 故乡) and 'In Memoriam' (*Shangshi* 伤逝). It can also be seen in 'The White-Haired Girl' (*Baimaonü* 白毛女) by He Jingzhi 贺敬之,[2] with its deep roots of nostalgia in rural China, in Zong Baihua's 宗白华 treatises on China's classical aesthetics, and in Qu Qiubai's research into Chinese myths and folk song traditions. Nostalgic utopia is not the same as nostalgia in Western culture; it is a particular phenomenon of the modernisation of Chinese culture. There are several important theoretical implications of nostalgic utopia:

1. The cultural basis for nostalgic utopia lies in traditional society; in the Daoist culture of idealising the past. Throughout the development of China, this has been, in the words of Lu Xun, 'the root of Chinese culture'.
2. The cultural expression 'nostalgic utopia' is based in 'harmony'. Harmony, *hexie* 和谐 in Chinese, has much more complexity of association than the English word. It is a 'sound from far away' and involves circularity and repetition of sound. Even where the foundations of the actual nation and the agrarian society have been shattered, there is still that cultural mechanism which provides Chinese people with an integrated emotional object. Through the mechanism of nostalgia the emotions of the Chinese people can be organised, and thus it underlays the process of modernisation. In Chinese society, this mechanism isn't a 'purification' but is a 'faraway' sound, a form of message left 'after departure'. As a theory, we propose calling it '*yu yun*' 余韵, a lingering resonance – a remainder of rhymes.
3. In the process of Chinese modernisation, almost at the same time that nostalgic utopia developed so too was introduced 'red utopia', which presents the values of socialism. Nostalgic utopia and red utopia have a structural relationship in the process of Chinese modernisation that is like the double-helix structure of DNA: the two structures of values are wrapped around each other in a dynamic relationship, each limiting the other. This characterises the underlying emotional structure of China's modernisation.

4. Literature and art in the process of the modernisation of Chinese society have been especially important because aesthetic appreciation is highly regarded in traditional Chinese culture. Literature and art have led the way. Since the outset of the twentieth century China has undergone a continuous series of 'aesthetic revolutions' – from the May Fourth Movement of 1919 and New Culture Movement of the 1910s and 1920s to the culture building of the Yan'an period; from the victory in the Korean War to the erupting of the Cultural Revolution between 1966 and 1976; from the 'Great Aesthetic Discussion' (*Meixue da taolun* 美学大讨论) of the 1980s through the first twenty years of the twenty-first century with the flourishing of Chinese art and cinema. The analysis of modern aesthetics in fact must be the analysis of the emotional structure of the development of China's modernisation.

The movie *Fang Hua* 芳华 (Youth), directed by Feng Xiaogang 冯小刚, was released in December 2017. The script is based on a book of the same name by Yan Geling 严歌苓, a Chinese writer who lives in the US. It attracted broad discussion and fierce disagreement among both academics and the general public in China. Some critics regarded it as a work of historical nihilism; some thought it was a product of the combination of capital and culture. Some articles praised it as a very high-quality modern Chinese movie, but others thought it was a cinematic expression of modern Cold War thought. The film is set in the period of the Sino-Vietnam War (1979) and is centred around the daily life, work, loves and betrayals of the young actors in the People's Liberation Army Southwest Military Division Military Song and Dance Troupe. The material is used to reflect on the complex relationship between society and literature and art during the forty years of reform and opening up. As a film about a song-and-dance troupe, it naturally contains a lot of song and dance, both rehearsal and performance. This serves not just as entertainment but also as material used to show how songs from different historical periods stimulate historical and cultural memory in contemporary Chinese culture. This chapter attempts to explain, in this complex cultural context, the meaning and mechanics of aesthetic response in *Fang Hua*.

NOSTALGIA IN *FANG HUA*

The widespread responses to *Fang Hua* were intense but conflicting. The divergence reflects obvious differences of sensibilities and the multi-layered character of China's contemporary society, as well as historical changes in aesthetic appreciation. The music of the opening and final scenes of film comes from an episode in the film *Xiao Hua* 小花 (Little Flower), made in 1979. In this way, the film links contemporary people's viewing experiences to a certain historical and cultural memory. A specific link is the song 'Rong Hua' 绒花 (Velvet Flower), whose lyrics include the following refrain:

In this world there is a beautiful flower
That is springtime
Clang, clang! Hard bone bursts open and the flower blooms
Drop by drop fresh blood dyes it red
Ah… Ah…
Velvet flower, velvet flower
Ah… Ah…
All along the road sweet fragrance covers the mountain cliffs.

The sequence in *Xiao Hua* that 'Rong Hua' accompanies shows a badly wounded People's Liberation Army (PLA) soldier being carried on a stretcher by guerrilla soldiers up a precipitous mountain path. In order to keep the stretcher level on the steep path, the female guerrilla leader must carry the stretcher from a crouching position. Sweat is pouring off her, blood is flowing from the wounded soldier, but resolutely, step by step, she keeps the stretcher stable until they deliver him to the field hospital at the top of the mountain. There, a love interest begins between the female guerrilla and the wounded soldier. This is paralleled in the poem's metaphor of cherry blossoms bursting forth from bare branches with the force of spring. The strength of love and the ideals of revolution release a huge energy. The distress that forces the cherry to produce such rich blossoms – 'all along the road sweet fragrance covers the mountain cliffs' – is mirrored in the triumph of the heroic rescue of the soldier. This scene from *Xiao Hua* undoubtedly has a very strong feeling of revolutionary romanticism.

The intertextuality, the overlay of *Xiao Hua* on *Fang Hua*, reveals a point of view and the director's aesthetic orientation. The distressed cherry is quite similar to the plum blossom flowering in winter, previously used as a central image by Mao Zedong 毛泽东 in his 1961 'Ode to the Plum Blossom – to the Tune of Bu Suan Zi' (*Bu Suanzi: Yongmei* 卜算子·咏梅) to praise beauty in adversity.

'Rong Hua' is an emotional song, filled with a burden of sorrow. From the point of view of aesthetics, *Fang Hua* is a work in the aesthetic style of 'nostalgia'. From the point of view of modern tragedy, *Fang Hua* uses the story of a young female 'artist-soldier' in a PLA song-and-dance troupe to give an account of the way utopian values have been part of China's revolutionary experience and how, in the context of market economics and consumerism, they are being negated and abandoned.

From the point of view of anthropological aesthetics, *Fang Hua* has two striking elements. The first is the design of the scenes and the sets. The monumental gateway which is the entrance to the military art troupe's base is a critical feature of the set; it is this structure which cuts off the world of the military art troupe from the world outside which is continually developing and changing, busy and bustling, filled with chaos, contradiction, suffering, and even the cruelty of war. Inside the monumental gateway of the art troupe we see beautiful young women – their thighs robust, their bodies graceful. There is lovely music and stirring dances, and a sense of the romantic love-longing of young girls. The whole scene is a modern version of the Peach Blossom Spring, an ancient tale of a beautiful utopia where, isolated from the outside world, people live an ideal life in harmony with nature (see Chapter 1). The monumental gateway is a ceremonial symbol, recurring in different episodes. It is first seen when the heroine, He Xiaoping 何小萍, arrives to become a dancer-soldier in the arts unit and again in her painful parting from the hero, Liu Feng 刘峰. Its solemn mausoleum decoration dates from the time of Mao Zedong's passing and is still standing, now old-fashioned, when Liu Feng returns crippled by war, exhausted and downtrodden from trying to make a living in the commercial free-for-all on Hainan Island. The once-glorious gateway, now a 'cultural relic', remains a silent witness to all the major occurrences and important developments of the plot. *Fang Hua* turns it into a modern altar, giving the military art troupe a special status. It is idealised and spiritualised – the time of youth, filled with blooming vitality, separated from the outside filled with struggle, war, blood, and filth. The troupe has served as a symbol of utopia – an enclave of art and beauty, seemingly safe from a painful world. Through the film Feng Xiaogang reveals the tragedy of China's passage into modernisation.

Secondly, the design of scenes and sets is complemented by the soundtrack. The songs sung by the characters in *Fang Hua* are mainly revolutionary songs from a different period of the modernisation of China's society, including, in addition to 'Velvet Flower', the typically triumphal 'The March of the PLA' (*Renmin Jiefangjun Jinxing Qu* 人民解放军进行曲), the theme of unity and friendship for minorities in 'The People's Soldier-Girl of the Grasslands' (*Caoyuan Nüminbin* 草原女民兵),[3] the patriotic mixture of Chinese traditional music and high-spirited folk song in 'Chairman Mao's Warriors are the Most Loyal to the Party' (*Mao Zhuxi de Zhanshi Zuiting Dang de Hua* 毛主席的战士最听党的话), 'Ode to Yi Meng' (*Yi Meng Song* 沂蒙颂) (discussed below), and 'Clothes-Washing Song' (*Xiyi Ge* 洗衣歌), with its theme about the PLA as brothers of the people bringing prosperity and happiness by washing their clothes (just as they had washed away outdated feudalistic thoughts and habits). Also included are 'Embroider a Golden Banner' (*Xiu Jinbian* 绣金匾) with its origin in anti-Japanese folk tunes but also composed to praise communist leaders such as Zhou Enlai 周恩来, 'Praising Heroes Song' (*Yingxiong Ernü* 英雄儿女) that laments young heroes dying on the battlefield of the Korean War, and 'Camel Bells' (*Tuo Ling* 驼铃), theme song of an anti-spy movie set at start of the Cultural Revolution. However, with the exception of original music written for the film, the soundtrack of *Fang Hua* is chosen mostly from a few highly emotional popular songs of the last forty years, including love songs sung by Deng Lijun, 'Farewell' by Li Shutong, the popular song 'Dense Emotion, Countless Threads', 'The Last Rose of Summer', and Western classical music from Tchaikovsky, Bach, and others. Throughout *Fang Hua* music and songs are important means for characterisation. From an aesthetic standpoint, the sound montage of *Fang Hua* is an important method of activating the viewers' cultural and historical memory.[4]

One of the aspects of China's modern aesthetic is that there is a recognition of the close relationship between art and ideology: the arts embody ideology and present it to audiences in a non-theoretical way that makes it comprehensible and appealing. This has made them very important in facilitating social change. *Fang Hua* has as its background the history of society through the period of transformation from the latter part of the Cultural Revolution to the full-scale engagement with market economics. The subject matter of the movie is taken from a particular cultural practice of managing the modernisation process – the Military Art Troupe (*Budui Wenyi Gongzuotuan* 部队文艺工作团). Two of the central themes of modernisation – revolution and nostalgia – are made clear through the love stories of three female soldiers. He Xiaoping, Xiao Suizi 萧穗子, and Lin Dingding 林丁丁 represent three different models of love: the self-sacrificing model, the realist model, and the narcissistic, self-serving model. The male hero, Liu Feng, is the living model of heroic behaviour, representative of red utopia. His tragedy is that he falls in love with the vain and exceedingly self-loving solo singer Lin Dingding. Liu Feng's life is tragically transformed when he attempts to embrace Lin Dingding, who has rejected his protestation of love; he falls from being the admired and selfless comrade who gives help wherever it is needed to someone who deserves to be disciplined.

In contrast to Liu Feng's early heroic status, He Xiaoping is mocked by her fellow dancers as lower class, which is signalled by her sweating heavily while dancing. Her father has been sentenced to a labour reform prison, her mother has remarried, she is bullied at home and receives no support, let alone personal warmth and care. Constant rejection makes her feel inferior and heavy-hearted, yet she is extremely diligent, using sacrifice and self-denial to preserve her fragile dignity. He Xiaoping is treated as an outsider from the moment she joins the art troupe – 'not one of us'. When they are practising the dance for 'Ode to Yi Meng', she is humiliated by the troupe – except for Liu Feng, who comes to her rescue. He displays traditional socialist values such as straightforwardness, kindness, willingness to help others, and self-sacrifice. The film positions Liu Feng and He Xiaoping in a way that gives them a positive value. However, as China's society is reshaped in the process of modernisation, these values win little respect. Even though in theory they are still the social ideals for mankind and standards for a finer human existence, in reality they have lost the role they should play in daily life; they have become alien, existing in quotation marks.

In terms of aesthetics, *Fang Hua* makes great use of red utopia songs in sound-and-image montages. For example, later in the film, He Xiaoping serves as a nurse in a field hospital which comes under disastrous attack and, following sustained trauma, she has a mental breakdown. She is brought out of her catatonic state when her former troupe performs 'Ode to Yi Meng' for her and her fellow mental patients, the same piece in which she had been humiliated. She steps out of the auditorium and, all alone in the moonlight, performs the dance – beautifully. The point is not just the effect of He Xiaoping being 'awakened' by the music but also the romantic revolutionary content of the song – in which the life of a severely wounded PLA soldier is saved by a young woman who expresses her milk for him. The 'Ode to Yi Meng' is based on a true story transformed into a work of art. It was also made into a ballet performed by the China Central Ballet in 1973, and in 1975 the Ba Yi Film Studio (Ba Yi Dianying Zhipianchang 八一电影制片厂) made it into a movie. Thus Feng Xiaogang uses the song as part of the plot but uses it also to present values of an earlier revolutionary era and offer a critique of the degenerate present.

CHINA'S MODERN AESTHETIC IN CONTEMPORARY ART

In China, contemporary art is a complex system of symbols and signposts. The complex cultural cyphers in historical and cultural memory generate new aesthetic meanings in the contemporary context, thereby becoming forerunners of a kind of aesthetic revolution and social change. Earlier we described the emotional structure of China's modern aesthetic as a dynamic double-helix structure: two interlocked elements – an aesthetic sense and a specific context that restricts and defines it – are interlocked. These two elements are red utopia and nostalgic utopia. They emerged at almost the same time in the process of China's social modernisation, but their character and emotional direction are very different. Red utopia and nostalgic utopia form a double-helix structure; they make up a huge emotional space filled with tension. Endless modernisation is accompanied by the constant problems and irritations of change, which people are able to withstand through an emotional aspect of spiritual belief that gives them courage and endurance. The tension of the double helix has produced a spiritual and emotional strength – '*tian xing jian*' 天行健 (from the commentaries to the *Book of Changes*) – a type of loftiness derived from China's traditional society. This also explains the cultural logic behind certain astonishing achievements of modernisation of China's society.

With reference to the distinctive nature of the modernisation of China's society, Li Zehou has described it as a twofold variation of initiation primer and national salvation: the particular situation of forcefully channelling the plan for the salvation of the Chinese people into the modernisation of China's society. This is without doubt accurate. Looking at it from the point of view of the two centuries of the process, particularly taking the experience and lessons learned from the last forty years of reform and opening up for reflecting on modern Chinese society, we believe that the aims of socialism are an important existing dimension, a theoretical expression of utopian existence. In 1516, in the early stages of the modernisation in England, the famous humanist Thomas More completed the book *Utopia*, which presented an imagined socialist society as a system more equitable, and more suited to human nature. In 1844 Karl Marx, while in Paris – that nineteenth-century capitalist capital city – wrote the famous *Paris Manuscripts.* The text analysed in depth the alienation of human nature and the disaster resulting from the capitalist mode of production and discussed how to stop alienation and pursue a system more in accord with human nature. Marx's philosophical and anthropological arguments remain very important in today's research in the field of humanism. In 2012, Shanghai Jiaotong University's School of Research into Aesthetics and Critical Theory and the editorial department of *Research on Marxist Aesthetics* and the School of Humanities of Manchester University hosted an international seminar on 'Marxism and Humanitarianism'. The papers were published in 2013 by the Central Editorial and Translating publishing house. Stemming from this seminar, a selection of writings from the participants was published by Pluto Press in 2017 as *For Humanism: Explorations in Theory and Politics.*

We believe that, from the point of view of Marxism, theoretical reflection on Chinese society's modernity and aesthetic modernity has three basic dimensions:

1. The inevitability of the historical phases of capitalist production, including the huge creative force of capitalist production; the inevitability of the alienation of human nature, the historical use of 'evil', and the foundation of the modern tragedy of society.
2. The historical inevitability of utopia, or the socialist objective, and the reasons why this has not yet come about, including the way this is presented in modern tragedy and the way it actually is in reality.
3. Traditional culture and historical memory and their role as a cultural symbol system, the way they are presented in contemporary society; with reference to the special quality of the theories about China's modernity, as a late developing 'third world' country but also as an ancient country with both a dazzlingly brilliant ancient culture and an 'unceasing self-improvement' gene, and the nostalgic utopia form this may take in the emotional structure of China's modernisation of culture. We believe the unique values of memory of past history, cultural tradition and the tragedy of human life reactivated in the context of contemporary society. Historical memory is a great force resisting capitalist modernisation, exploring not just individual self-improvement, but the cultural form of the great re-awakening of the entire nation.

Looking at China in comparison with the UK, the distinctiveness of China's aesthetic modernity has three main aspects:

First, although England went through the Renaissance and religious reformation, in the journey to modernisation Protestantism and Catholicism both had widespread influence; religious belief to varying degrees still supported people's spiritual world during the modernising process. By comparison, in China's development, modern production methods and many kinds of institutions of modern society came into society through violent intervention.

From the Opium Wars to the Sino-Japanese War, China's civilization and its empire were repeatedly assaulted and humiliated by the industrialised imperialist big powers. However, faced with the powerful and irresistible pressures of modernisation, Chinese culture did not completely collapse or completely lose hope. A compassionate and unyielding spirit and emotional strength bound together the Chinese nation; we call this concept 'tragic humanism'. The basis for its appearance is the tragedy of the modernisation process of developing countries and the people of those countries but, by contrast, its cultural gene is this kind of lofty tragic spirit expressed in Chinese classical texts, for example, from the *Book of Changes*: 'Heaven, in its motion, gives the idea of strength. The superior man, in accordance with this, strives for self-improvement.' In outstanding works like 'Farewell' by Li Shutong, 'Wild Grass' (*Yecao* 野草) by Lu Xun, 'Qin Yuan Spring – Snow' (*Qinyuan Chun: Xue* 沁园春·雪) by Mao Zedong, 'Yellow River Chorus' (*Huanghe Song* 黄河颂) by Xian Xinghai 冼星海, 'White Deer Yuan' (*Bailu Yuan* 白鹿原) by Chen Zhongshi 陈忠实, 'Ordinary World' (*Pinfan de Shijie* 平凡的世界) by Lu Yao 路遥, and the movies *Yellow Earth* (*Huang Tudi* 黄土地), *The Assassin* (*Jinke Ci Qin Wang* 荆轲刺秦王), *Lily* (*Baihe* 百合), and so on, this spirit and culture still endure. These are proof of the humanitarian and spiritual level that the Chinese nation is capable of attaining through art.

Second, the basis for the industrial revolution in the UK was the development of market economics and progress in science and technology. Economics, physics, and biology as subjects for study occupied a central position and performed a leading function in the early stages of capitalism in the UK. In China, the progress of society's modernisation started from transformations in literature, the arts, and culture. Surveyed generally, in the course of the modernisation of China's society, literature and the arts have guided the transformation and development, have occupied a central position, and have performed a leading function. In the outburst of the May Fourth Movement, the Yan'an Forum on Art and Literature held during the Anti-Japanese War, the subsequent 'Yan'an Literature and Art Phenomenon', the literature and arts work groups of the Korean War period, the 'New Folk Song Movement' of the Great Leap Forward, the explosive flourishing during the early period of reform and opening up, right up to the recent 'China Dream' and its great revival of the Chinese nation we can see the obvious phenomenon of the tremendous development of China's society. As well as serving as a prophet of transformation, literature and art provided extremely important value standards for a society in transformation. One could say they were a spiritual backbone.

Thirdly, relating to the progress of the modernisation of society in the UK, Engels, in *The Condition of the Working Class in England*, and Marx, in *Economic and Philosophic Manuscripts of 1844* and *Capital*, give detailed and profound analyses. In this process, individualism, cold calculation, and the pursuit of material pleasure became the main features of British society and culture. By comparison, in the process of the modernisation of China's society, because of the great trauma of war and great cultural trauma, at a time when neighbouring Japan had already successfully modernised, China was in a situation which was incomparably depressing, with a past that it was unbearable to look back upon. For this reason, struggling to get out of its predicament, the country put all its hope in the future. This is another special characteristic of China's social modernisation process. It was an opportune moment for a positive view, red utopia, to take hold. It was disseminated rapidly in China and had an extensive and powerful influence. It was also in this sense that holding fast to China's traditional culture and criticising the production methods of capitalism brought about the model and produced the growth of what we have called nostalgic utopia and aesthetic modernity in China's culture in the twentieth century. From 'Farewell' by Li Shutong, 'In Memoriam' by Lu Xun, and 'Border City' (*Bian Cheng* 边城) by Shen Congwen 沈从文 to 'White Deer Yuan' by Cheng Zhongshi, 'Ordinary World' by Lu Yao, and 'Me and the Altar to the Earth' (*Wo yu Ditan* 我与地坛) by Shi Tiesheng 史铁生, to the movies *Yellow Earth*, *The Good Person of the Three Gorges* (*Sanxia Haoren* 三峡好人), *The Woman Sesame Oil Maker* (*Xianghun Nü* 香魂女), *Er Mo* 二嫫, and *Lily* by Zhou Xiaowen 周晓文, right up the movie we are analysing here, we believe that, within the emotional structure of China's aesthetic modernity, red utopia and nostalgic utopia are combined together in a double-helix structure. The two are bound together – they are complementary, but sometimes clashing in contradiction, making the utopian space dynamic and a space of relative autonomy, a utopia that is humane and has real emotions and as a result has great strength.

In *Fang Hua*, if we say that the female artist-soldier in the bloom of youth is an expression of nostalgic utopia then the military cultural work group is indeed a huge red utopia machine; if we say that the young woman's first love is nostalgic utopia then the 'Living Lei Feng' (*huo Lei Feng* 活雷锋) Freudian-style love is a distorted red utopia.[5] If we say the songs 'Velvet Flower', 'Farewell', 'Yimeng Ode', and 'The Last Rose of Summer' are expressions of nostalgic utopia, then 'The People's Soldier-Girl of the Grasslands', 'Clothes-Washing Song', 'Embroider a Golden Banner', 'Praising Heroes Song', and 'Seeing Off a Comrade-in-Arms' are indeed artistic expressions of red utopia. In *Fang Hua*, these two types of utopia, with different types of image and narrative, make up different sound-and-image montages, effectively expressing highly complex essential elements of real life within that specific context.

It is worth paying attention in the movie: we can observe the creators criticising and poking fun at Lei Feng, a typical figure from a specific historical context (one of the best known of the cultural heroes of the communist revolution, and the central figure in many propaganda posters). In the movie Liu Feng is a collective-minded, exceptional person and an 'honest fellow' from that period, but in the social relationships after reform and opening up he becomes an 'unclean person' and a scapegoat,[6] and becomes the exiled partner. This is an era when economics and development lead the way, a tragedy where red utopia itself has been called into question. The liberator has dramatically taken up the position of the person being liberated. From the viewpoint of history, the tragedy in this is a typical case, worthy of thorough analysis.

TRAGIC HUMANISM IN CHINA

Concerning the understanding of tragic humanism, we tend to rely on two of Karl Marx's arguments as a basis. One is an analysis of 'modern tragedy', the other is Marx's theoretical explanation of 'the laws of beauty'. These two theoretical rules govern our understanding of China's modern tragic humanism within the Marxist scope.

In the *Economic and Philosophic Manuscripts of 1844*, when Marx was discussing his understanding of what future society is best suited to human nature, he produced an argument in the philosophical-anthropological sense concerning a whole series of questions about the criteria under which human freedom and liberation can actually come about. Marx wrote:

> Admittedly animals also produce. They build themselves nests, dwellings, like the bees, beavers, ants, etc. But an animal only produces what it immediately needs for itself or its young. It produces one-sidedly, whilst man produces universally. It produces only under the dominion of immediate physical need, whilst man produces even when he is free from physical need and only truly produces in freedom therefrom. An animal produces only itself, whilst man reproduces the whole of nature. An animal's product belongs immediately to its physical body, whilst man freely confronts his product. An animal forms things in accordance with the standard and the need of the species to which it belongs, whilst man knows how to produce in accordance with the standard of every species, and knows how to apply everywhere the inherent standard to the object. Man therefore also forms things in accordance with the laws of beauty.[7]

The existence of the 'laws of beauty' informs us that humankind can mould its own image according to the laws of beauty. Yet it is only when we mould our own livelihood that we can, in the truest sense, gain liberation. It is exactly in this sense that I disagree with the value basis of Feng Xiaogang and Yan Geling. Feng and Yan believe that in this modern society it would not be possible for Lei Feng to exist. In this context Lei Feng would be a product of falsehood or pretence. However, Marx believes in special contexts and conditions, whether or not one can 'according to the laws of beauty' carry out an activity where you yourself act in a dignified way. In the sense of philosophic anthropology, this is exactly the criterion by which to judge whether one is a person who has reached a state of freedom and liberation. In this way, we are not only above animals but also above people in positions of power and 'the beautiful people'. It is also the place where people have meaning and true flashes of enlightenment as people. In *Fang Hua*, Liu Feng and He Xiaoping are just that type of person, but they are both either abandoned or humiliated by their own relatives, comrades-in-arms, and people of attractive appearance. While they still approach the world and the people and events around them with hearts filled with love, the 'emotional structure' is actually 'tragic humanism'.

Marx's theoretical rules about tragic humanism are put forward in a letter he wrote to Ferdinand Lassalle, one of the leaders of international communism, in April 1859. In order to express his revolutionary ideas but also to spread the ideas about tragic values which he regarded as important, Lassalle wrote a tragedy, *Franz von Sickingen*. Marx wrote with reference to the theoretical questions raised by this work:

> The implicit conflict is just not tragic; it is the tragic conflict upon which the revolutionary party of 1848–49 justly foundered. Hence making it the fulcrum of a modern tragedy can only meet with my wholehearted approval, But then I ask myself, is the theme in question suitable for the portrayal of that conflict? . . . This would have enabled you to give expression in a far greater measure precisely to the most modern ideas in their most unsophisticated form; whereas in fact now the dominant idea, apart from religious freedom, is civic unity. Then you would automatically have had to 'Shakespeare' more, whereas your principal failing is, to my mind, 'Schillering' i.e. using individuals as mere mouthpieces for the spirit of the times.

In this letter, Marx explains his understanding of 'modern tragedy' – that is, the imperatives of history, and the tragic contradictions that make it temporarily impossible for these imperatives to be realised. In addition, Marx gives his own opinions about the way in which this modern tragedy is represented. We believe because the aesthetic experience itself includes the extremely complex contradictions of life and living, so long as the artist has the courage to face their own internal world, and sincerely face the world they live in, and express themselves from the material of their perceptions of aesthetic experience of contemporary real life, not being influenced by any 'spirit of the age' preconceived notions or ideological restrictions, there is a possibility, using the most unsophisticated form, of representing the most modern thinking, and expressing a humanist tragedy with contemporary aesthetic meaning.

First, let's have a look at why Feng Xiaogang could be considered the mouthpiece of a certain spirit of this age of possessive individualism. The scene of the art troupe rehearsing the dance to 'Ode to Yi Meng' comes up many times, encompassing the entire course of the tragic quality of He Xiaoping's life.

The first time is during a rehearsal of a dance accompaniment to 'Ode to Yi Meng'. This is a number in which two actors, a female and a male, act as a pair; it requires close physical co-operation between them as well as emotional communication and cohesion. However, what He Xiaoping comes up against is passive resistance from her partner. The director, when she sees this – an act completely contrary to the theme and spirit of the number – criticises the male actor. She is confronted by his refusal to perform, and orders another male actor to take his place, which results in another refusal. The company is a military arts troupe, part of the army, and refusing an order is a major act of insubordination. The entire male contingent of the performance team completely lack discipline, and they reply derisively to the troupe leader. This is undoubtedly a disastrous blow for He Xiaoping. At this moment, Liu Feng, released from service as an actor because of a back injury, offers to partner her. Liu Feng is attempting to rescue the rehearsal and the performance, but it is also giving forceful support to the fragile soul and emotional stability of He Xiaoping.

The second time we hear 'Ode to Yi Meng' is during a rest period in the empty rehearsal hall. Liu Feng and He Xiaoping are humming the song as they practise the dance. As Liu Feng is performing a lift of the slight He Xiaoping, his injured back gives out and they fall over, but he still insists on completing the rehearsal.

The third time we hear 'Ode to Yi Meng' is long after Liu Feng and He Xiaoping have both (separately) had to leave the art troupe. Both have since been through intensely, bloody combat. Liu Feng, though badly wounded, still bravely shielded a fellow soldier; He Xiaoping, a nurse in a field hospital, tending the wounded with utmost care and feeling, covers a dying young soldier with her body during an air raid. In the film it is immediately after this that 'Ode to Yi Meng' plays. Its accompanying dance appears on the screen, the first time we see it in a formal performance. The location is the big assembly hall of the military district which Liu Feng and He Xiaoping both liked very much, but neither Liu Feng nor He Xiaoping appears in this performance. The performance on the stage is magnificent, a triumph of youth – the female actor is beautiful and warm, the male actor is heroic, handsome, and forceful; it's a performance where the content and the style both achieve completeness. However, the audience – the heroes and the wounded – are unmoved, their faces without expression, some even dropping off to sleep.

But the melody of the song moves He Xiaoping deeply. She is now already a catatonic mental patient, and while the tune is playing, she slowly gets up, and goes out onto the lawn outside the assembly hall, stretches her body and dances unrestrainedly, lost in an endless daydream. We have every reason to believe the He Xiaoping of this moment is happy, free, with a contented heart. In summary she has fulfilled the 'rules of beauty'.

In the movie, under Feng Xiaogang's direction, the dance 'Ode to Yi Meng' has been completely formalised and aestheticised and has become a kind of voicing of the spirit of the age. The historical facts behind the origins of 'Ode to Yi Meng', the historical army and the relationship between the PLA fighters and the people of the old base area are not shown, and the historical fact of the sacrifice, dedication, and love of the Liu Fengs and He Xiaopings striving for the sake of lofty ideals are not shown. All the passion of the magnificent 'Ode to Yi Meng' dance has faded into history. Even so, the song 'Ode to Yi Meng' continues to be heard and has animated countless Liu Fengs and He Xiaopings, enabling them to experience a tragic humanism.

The tight double-helix structure of red utopia and nostalgic utopia, for the audience and for the people who in reality are ceaselessly confronting the hardships of fate, offers up rich content; there is the beauty of real understanding between people, willingness to help, caring, dedication – or, you could say, love filled with humanity. When a work of art causes actual appreciators and critics of this type of aesthetic experience to appear, we say tragic humanism has been born.

Fang Hua provides two revelations. First, in the process of the modernisation of China's society, because of the particular characteristics of the transformation, and because of the special characteristics of China's culture, the aesthetic modernity of China has its own special features. From the point of view of cultural anthropology and aesthetics, there exist in China's traditional society very strong cultural rituals which even today still have extremely important functions. Therefore, when we are analysing contemporary movies and art, we need to give full expression to the special characteristics of China's culture and the great strength of cultural rituals. In Chinese history, the tradition of behavioural norms is a very strong ritualistic tradition, including the Ming Dynasty philosopher Wang Yangming 王阳明 who emphasises the 'inner tradition' of *xin xue* 心学 (study of the heart). Its essence is a 'soul rite', an 'emotional rite', and emotion of what we call 'tragic humanism' arises spontaneously.

Secondly, the mechanism of expression in China's culture is more inclined towards the aural. For this reason, research into China's aesthetic modernity pays particular attention to China's folk songs, traditional music, and song dramas which, for the most part, have music as their basic mechanism of expression. Although frequently by the end there is a 'happy ending', most of them use tunes that stir compassion. Speaking from the anthropological point of view, Chinese culture also has the tradition of liking '*renao*' 热闹, the 'happy occasion', but in Chinese culture '*nao*' (noise) is usually offset against a more innate melancholy. The essence of the sadness does not have its basis in religious belief, but in the belief that people have in human nature – a form of tragic humanism.

In conclusion, we have taken the movie *Fang Hua* as an illustration of several aspects of China's aesthetic modernity, including the possibility of the re-establishment of tragic humanism within contemporary culture. Preliminary analysis and discussion suggest we can form the following initial conclusions:

1. In research into Chinese aesthetic modernity and contemporary emotional structure, the theoretical methods of aesthetic anthropology are of primary importance.

2. As far as contemporary Chinese art is concerned, the essential 'code' of aesthetic modernity's double-helix-like structure lies in cultural memory. The old songs of traditional culture and of the 'red classic' repertoire demonstrate this double helix-structure.
3. In the emotional structure of China's modern aesthetics, tragic humanism is of utmost importance, and critically important in addressing contemporary artistic production in China.

NOTES

1. Li Shutong (1880–1942) was a Chinese pioneer in aesthetic education with a Buddhist background. He was widely known as Hongyi, his Buddhist name.
2. 'The White-Haired Girl' is a Chinese libretto by He Jingzhi, based on the folklore of the Shanxi–Chahar–Hebei border region. The plot is centred around the fate of peasant women suffering under imperialism that are later rescued by the communists.
3. A song from Mongolia (or at least in the Mongolian style) in the 1975 movie *Flowers in a Riot of Colour*. The message is that all the racial minorities, or at least the female members, are a big, happy family.
4. As a notable technique used in *Fang Hua*, the sound montage consists of songs popular during the 1946–1949 War of Liberation, the Cultural Revolution, and the early stage of reform and opening up. The sound montage links concurrent social and life experiences of the audience with experiences of the above historical periods, hence the evocative power that reactivates memories of the past.
5. Lei Feng (1940–1962) was a PLA soldier and a CCP propaganda model of loyalty and service; 'living Lei Feng' is a phrase widely used in China to describe anyone that has showcased a spirit of selfless service.
6. In the conventional Chinese society in which the movie is set, touching a woman outside of one's family is considered almost a crime. Having committed this 'crime' the male character becomes a social outcast. It is also notable that the only exceptions are the children of upper-class government leaders – they are privileged to have more intimate interactions with the opposite sex, as shown in the 1994 film *In the Heat of the Sun* (*Yangguang Canlan de Rizi* 阳光灿烂的日子).
7. Karl Marx, *Economic and Philosophic Manuscripts of 1844* (Moscow: Foreign Languages Publishing House, 1961), 75–76.

5
American Dreams in China: The Case of *Zhongguo Hehuoren*

Qinghong Yin

The film *Zhongguo Hehuoren* by the Hong Kong director Peter Hosan Chan (Chen Kexin), released in mainland China in May 2013, achieved huge and unexpected commercial success – its box-office receipts surpassed RMB 500 million within one month. The Chinese title translates literally as 'The Chinese Partners' but the English title – *American Dreams in China* – better characterises the story of three Peking University students in the 1980s who have an 'American Dream'. Failing in their attempt to fulfil their ambitions in the US, they create a version of the American Dream in China: they set up an English language school, New Dreams, that becomes very successful. Unsurprisingly, the critics saw the film as the director's commentary on Xi Jinping's 'China Dream' and its ideology, and this produced much discussion of the China Dream and the American Dream.[1] The China Dream was introduced by Xi Jinping on 15 November 2012, on a visit to the *Road to Revitalisation* exhibition at the National Museum of China.[2] At that time Xi was only general secretary of the Communist Party of China (CPC), but on 17 March 2013 he was elected national chairman, and he used the expression 'China Dream' nine times in his acceptance speech. China Dream has obviously become a central concept of the CPC under Xi's leadership. The concept of the China Dream was rapidly disseminated throughout the CPC and the country, and a great tide of 'China Dreaming' swept over all Chinese society. The China Dream remains very much topical and writers and artists have produced diverse versions of the China Dream. This chapter takes *Zhongguo Hehuoren* as a case study, analysing the connotations, intentions, and values expressed in the China Dream and questioning the patterns of behaviour it displays.

WHY THE CHINA DREAM?

The main character of *Zhongguo Hehuoren* is Cheng Dongqing (played by Huang Xiaoming), the son of a peasant family living in poverty. After years of student hardship, he finally gets a place to study foreign languages at Peking University. At university he becomes sworn friends with Meng Xiaojun (played by Deng Zhao), who comes from a wealthier family with a tradition of overseas study, and also with Wang Yang (played by Tong Dawei), a young man with literary aspirations. In common with many other university students, they share an ambition to go to the US. Meng Xiaojun is the only one to succeed in getting a visa and he goes off to the US to study. Cheng Dongqing becomes an English teacher at Peking University, but he is dismissed from his post for illegally earning money by giving private tuition. There is plenty of demand for English tuition and he and Wang Yang set up an English language school that rapidly makes them a lot of money. At the same time, Meng Xiaojun, studying in the US, has not achieved the success he had anticipated. At first, he works as an assistant in a biological laboratory, responsible for raising white mice, but when he loses his job to another Chinese student, he can find work only as a busboy in a restaurant. Finally, with his American Dream shattered and having difficulty making ends meet, he decides there is no option but to go back home. Back in China, he joins Cheng Dongqing's language school, and the three good friends are again together. Working together, they manage to transform the school into the New Dream Group, and to become the first educational enterprise from China to trade on the New York Stock Exchange – they have realised their personal dreams of success.

It is obvious that the China Dream the film is talking about is first and foremost a dream of individual economic success – more specifically, the success achieved by onetime losers. The three characters have all been losers in some respects. Cheng Dongqing is born into a poor family and fails his entrance exam twice before getting into Peking University. He is repeatedly refused a visa to study in the US.

At university he falls in love but through being conscientious about his studies and through his own easygoing nature, he loses his girlfriend when she decides not to return from study in the US. He loses his teaching job by breaking the rules – thereby failing in his profession. Wang Yang succeeds in his application for a visa but because his American girlfriend wants to stay in China he declines it. And when she returns to the US four years later, he is abandoned – losing both his love and his dream of the US. He is a would-be poet, but no publisher is willing to publish his work. In despair, with shattered dreams, he burns his poems, cuts off his long hair, and has no choice but to join Cheng Dongqing's English school. Meng Xiaojun, similarly, his hopes crushed, finds Cheng's school a way out. The film shows how the three failures working as a united team (*tuanjie*) and through conscientious struggle turn an English school into China's largest commercial education group, and achieve huge personal success.

This kind of loser-makes-good story usually wins a heartfelt emotional response from the general public because, in reality, people who fail are in the majority, and success is their dream. Meng Xiaodong wants Cheng Dongqing to give a lecture on the subject of aspirational dreams. Meng tells Cheng there is no one who could talk more convincingly about dreams than him, a failure who is now the head of a school. In his lecture, Cheng Dongqing says that it is more likely that Chinese students will fail than any other students in the world because they are faced with the most ruthless exam system in the world. From primary to middle school, high school, university, and even in overseas study, there are very few students who achieve the grades they need for success in the system; most students are losers. Failure is everywhere, human life feels that hopeless. But there is a saying that if you jump into the water, you won't drown if you just keep swimming. If you just tread water, that's when you drown. There's nothing scary about failure, it's only the fear of failure that is really scary. The only thing we can do is find victory from failure and hope in despair. His lecture is very appealing, giving the students an injection of 'dream stimulant' while they were experiencing the reality of ruthlessness and pressure. He is loudly applauded. The film tells the audience that even though their previous American Dream has failed, the 'China Dream' can be realised. This was an important factor in the film's great box office success.

Of course, even though *Zhongguo Hehuoren* has as its model the pioneering example of New Oriental Education and Technology Group, and has a strong biographical flavour, it is not the story of any one particular person's or company's journey; rather it reflects the story of the struggles of countless Chinese people in the last forty years of reform and opening up. Therefore, the China Dream shared by a generation of Chinese people can be seen as the dream of becoming rich. At the end of the film the director runs a slideshow of successful Chinese business people, for example Liu Chuanzhi of Lenovo, Wang Shi of Vanke and Ma Yun of Alibaba. They are shown both at the start of their business career and after they had attained success under the title 'their story, perhaps it's also your story', using visual effects in the style of children's programmes and accompanied by the 1970s hit 'The Story of Time' (*Guangyin de Gushi*). The director, Peter Chan, has said that *Zhongguo Hehuoren* is absolutely not a propaganda movie for New Orient, nor is it a biopic of New Orient; its subject matter is, rather, thirty years of the shared experience of the Chinese people.[3] What the film wants to tell the audience is that during China's reform and opening up there have been countless Chinese people of all kinds, particularly those from modest backgrounds, who have failed but who, through their own creative efforts and struggles, have in the end achieved that communal dream of getting rich.

As I see it, the China Dream related in the film is not solely the dream of personal success and societal enrichment. It can also be seen as the dream of the resurgence of the Chinese people; this is a major factor in the success of the film. At the same time as telling the story of the three main characters going together from failure to success, it puts before the viewer the huge transformation that Chinese society has been through and its changed customs and fashions. Through the film, we can see the course of the changes brought about by economic development in Chinese society since the 1980s; major events such as the restoration of the college entrance exams, reform and opening up, and the US bombing of the Chinese embassy in Yugoslavia. We see the craze for overseas study and individuals leaving employment in the state sector to start private businesses. We see KFC arriving in China, shareholder ownership reforms, enterprises raising money through the stock market, the constraints on small private enterprise in a rigid system, and so on. The changes in ideology and emotional attachments of Chinese people over the past forty years are displayed in the film. While the audience is appreciating the story of the success of the underdog, they also experience China becoming rich and strong, and the tremendous strength of the Chinese people. I am of the opinion that the film is a highly politicised form of entertainment, whose success is closely related to current political attitudes.

Fredric Jameson's concept of the 'fable of nationality' can help us better understand *Zhongguo Hehuoren*. When discussing the literature of the 'Third World', Jameson said (in the Chinese translation of *Postmodernism, or, the Cultural Logic of Late Capitalism*), 'All writings in the Third World have fables and exceptional characteristics: we should read these writings as National Fables.' This is because 'Third World writings, even those which appear to be about individuals and rushed along by libido, always project a kind of politics through National Fable: stories about the fortunes of individuals contain fables of mass culture of the third world, and shocks to society.'[4] This is to say, even though this script is relating an individual company's story, it is always a metaphor for the nation-state's political ideology. Even though Jameson is only taking the works of Lu Xun as examples, and characterising the entire literature of the Third World as 'National Fable' style, this is undoubtedly one-sided. However, to a certain extent, using the 'National Fable' concept to interpret some contemporary Chinese literature and artistic writings can be productive. *Zhongguo Hehuoren* can also be seen as a 'national fable' of modern China's gradual rise to prominence.[5] It not only tells the story of the success of the countless small individual businesses in Chinese society of the last forty years, the process of the huge changes and China's rise as an economic force, it is also a metaphor for the way in which, suffering from Western colonialist incursions since 1840, the Chinese people historically had the dream of striving for a better future, pursuing national resurgence, and national wealth and strength. The China Dream is not only the dream of personal success; it is linked together with the great dream of the resurgence of the entire Chinese people. As Xi Jinping has said, 'This dream is the condensing together the long-held wish of several generations of Chinese people; it embodies the benefit of the entire Chinese nation and the Chinese people; it is what every son and daughter of China looks forward to. History tells us that the future fortunes of every person is intimately bound to the future fortunes of the country and the race.'[6] On this basis, with Xi Jinping at its heart, the CPC has stated its governing motive to be 'one China Dream, two centenary goals'. By the time the first centenary arrives – when China reaches the hundredth anniversary of the founding of CPC in 2021 – a 'relatively comfortable' society will be fully in place. By the second centenary, the hundredth anniversary of the founding of the PRC in 2049, China will have built a strong, democratic, civilised, compassionate, modern socialist country. And so, the China Dream which *Zhongguo Hehuoren* relates to can be understood not just as the dream of the success of an individual enterprise or of society getting rich; it is also the dream of the resurgence of the Chinese people. Jameson said, 'the fable in Third World culture, when it relates to the experiences of individuals interacting with each other, always includes the narrative of the difficulties experienced by the entire body itself'.[7] *Zhongguo Hehuoren* very skilfully mingles the experiences of the individual and the collective historical memory; it expresses the imaginative freedom of the small enterprise, at the same time as being symptomatic of the structure of the emotional feelings of the collective, in this way moving countless viewers, and achieving box office success.

THE VALUE CONFLICT EMBEDDED IN THE CHINA DREAM

Xi Jinping, when talking of the China Dream, has said that the 'China Dream is a national dream, it is also the dream of each Chinese person. The root of the China Dream is, after all, the people's dream, it has to be realised by close reliance on the people, it must unceasingly bring benefit to the people.'[8] What is the core value of the China Dream? What is the core value concept of Chinese society? These are topics which cannot be avoided when discussing the theoretical connotations and the value dimensions of the China Dream. From the point of view of the values expressed in *Zhongguo Hehuoren* there is no doubt that China is currently in a confused period, a void of values.[9] In the forty years of reform and opening up, a great number of societal values have emerged in China, but at the same time, the central values of society should not be lost amongst the profusion. There are many conflicting values contained in the China Dream of the film; this is the main reason why it attracted so many opposing criticisms and discussions.

First, there is the conflict between the China Dream and traditional Chinese values. The title of the film – *Zhongguo Hehuoren* – refers to the enterprise cooperation pattern of friends working together to build a Chinese-style business and finally becoming successful. Since its release it has attracted heated discussion about the model of the 'Chinese-style business partner'. No matter whether it is in traditional Chinese society, or in the last forty years, the age of reform and opening up, this model of the 'Chinese-style business partner' is an extremely common occurrence; it very much typifies and embodies Chinese people's values and ways of thinking. The most important characteristic of this type of cooperation is to build a business in partnership with your most trusted friends: a style of friendship where brothers will live or die together is a prerequisite and the foundation. In the film, Cheng Dongqing, Meng Xiaojun, and Wang Yang are three university friends. They live and study together, they take huge risks for one another's sake, they have bloody fights with each other, give each other dumb ideas and chase after girls, and as a result have deep comradeship almost like brothers – friends through thick and thin. Chinese-style partnerships advocate the value of proper behaviour over personal advantage; being happy together with friends is enough. Everyone feels, as the saying has it, that 'if you've got wealth share it, if you're in difficulty carry it together, eat big chunks of meat, drink big glasses of liquor'. One scene displays this attitude clearly: when Cheng Dongqing first earns serious money, he divides it very roughly in half by the thickness of each stack of notes. He hands over one stack to Wang Yang who doesn't even count the money but yells out happily, 'we're rich', and throws it in the air. This method of sharing out money is a typical example illustrating the trust, comradeship, and emotional thought without calculation between Chinese-style business partners. This kind of cooperation is profoundly influenced by the traditional culture of classical Chinese novels such as *The Water Margin* (*Shuihu Zhuan*) and *The Romance of Three Kingdoms* (*Sanguo Yanyi*). In traditional Chinese society this was a very widespread phenomenon.

However, in the process of the modernising of China, the development of a market economy has inevitably brought in new values; individualist attitudes have received affirmation and encouragement. Thus, a conflict between the modern values based on personal advantage and traditional values that at their core place proper behaviour above profit is inevitable. The contradiction inherent in the Chinese-style business partnership is bound to erupt. There is the view that 'even brothers should be clear about money', but how then to deal with brotherly camaraderie and at the same time be clear about money? This really depends on the people involved. Some people put emphasis on consideration for other people's feelings and are embarrassed to fight for their personal advantage, whereas others will not give an inch when it comes to advantage and profit.

There is also conflict between camaraderie and regulations. Emphasis on friendship is a premise of Chinese-style partnerships, the emotional basis for attaching importance to friends undergoing hardships and struggles together, emphasis on shared experience, cronyism, and taking into consideration hard work even if it is ineffective. However, the values of modern enterprises place greater emphasis on rules, systems, and merit-based appointment, and they lay stress on efficiency, impartiality, and principle. For example, in the film, Meng Dongsheng, who has taken on board Western-style thinking, suggests to Cheng Dongqing that he should fire their employee Zhang Yi, because not only is he a bad teacher, but also he will not accept training, and opposes new teaching methods. But Cheng Dongqing regards Zhang Yi as a founding member, having worked with them from when they operated in a disused factory, so he can't be dismissed, and he suggests that he is moved from a teaching position to office management. Meng Xiaojun replies if his work is not good, he is not suddenly going to improve (*bu jiang fan sheng*), and if Cheng doesn't even have the courage to dismiss an employee, how can he be the boss of a company? The notion of what is involved in company development or in regulating a system – for example, whether or not to take the company public – is the kind of problem that constantly results in arguments between Meng and Cheng. Wang Dan, at his own wedding ceremony, presents his friends with three pieces of heartfelt advice: never play mahjong with your mother-in-law, never go to bed with a woman who is cleverer than you, and whatever you do don't start up a company with your best friends. This joke is the conclusion he has reached through his experience of Chinese-style partnerships. After the friends and relatives have all departed, with the help of a lot of wine, the three good friends pour out their deepest feelings, many years of forbearance, misunderstandings, constraints, pointing out their grievances with one another. Finally they have a big fight, and a crying session, a thorough bust-up, and the next day they go their separate ways. However, facing an accusation by the American EES of publishing pirated teaching materials, Meng and Wang decide to come back again, to help Cheng. Faced with a challenge to the well-being of the company, the good friends reunite, go to the US for negotiations, and successfully complete the public listing of New Dream. The three principal characters, after experiencing the sweetness of the early stages of working together, then a middle period of friction, conflict, fighting, and even separation, have finally come together again. Their mutual trust and friendship restored, they hope the language school will develop into something really big. They grasp each other's hands and head for success. They have transformed New Dream and realised their individual China Dream.

Yet there is a question of how much the film reflects real life. In real life many people who set up partnerships initially based on friendships end up growing apart because of the unequal distribution of benefits, or even have a falling out and become enemies. How to deal with friendly relationships in a reasonable way and at the same time still be able to maintain individual distribution of profits is still a major problem confronting the China-style partnership.

Second, there is the conflict between the China Dream and the traditional values of socialism. From 1949, when the CPC came to power, up to 1978, the mainstream values of socialism in the new China were high levels of collectivism, advocating the spirit of selfless contribution in the service of the people. However, since reform and opening up, radical changes have happened to these traditional socialist values. In the film, when Cheng Dongqing first finds employment after university, his leader, Director Gao, asks him to give his nephew extra English tuition. After Cheng Dongqing has done this for a while, he raises the matter of fees with the director. Director Gao replies, 'Do you know why I asked you to help out? It's because you are a sincere and kind person. A school is not a marketplace. If there is payment, the character of the thing changes.' In the end he gives him some leftover dumplings to show his gratitude. In Director Gao's view the extra English tuition is unselfish help between associates; fees should not be mentioned. If money is mentioned, feelings are hurt. Cheng, on the contrary, expects to be rewarded for his work, but because Director Gao is a leader, he dare not demand payment; all he can do is mutter under his breath, 'Other people take a leap into the ocean, I put dumplings into a pot of boiling water.'[10] When the school finally dismisses Cheng from his post for making money by giving lessons outside the school, Director Gao, as leader, displays a strict impartiality; he ignores their past relationship and doesn't intervene. From this, we can see that under the impact of the new values brought in by market economics resigning and jumping into the ocean becomes departure from collectivism. The tide of the age is to pursue personal gain; individual profit will take precedence over benefits for other people and collective benefit every time.

At the beginning of reform and opening up, some highly fashionable slogans characterised the new values of Chinese society: 'No matter if the cat is white or black, so long as it is good at catching mice'; 'Time is money, efficiency is life'; 'Learn maths and physics and the whole world holds no fears'; 'Cross the river by feeling for stones' (i.e., look before you leap). All these reflect from different angles the new values in Chinese society. Therefore, in the process of realising the China Dream, this tendency to follow new values was bound to create conflict with the traditional socialist values. Fewer people pursued spiritual values and ideological beliefs; many more people were pursuing material benefits. Fewer and fewer people worked hard, were diligent and thrifty, whereas the numbers swelled of those who were wilfully extravagant and pursued only their own pleasure.

THE CONFLICT BETWEEN THE CHINA DREAM AND THE AMERICAN DREAM

Throughout the modernisation of China, the US was an object of study and at the same time was also the competitor. At the outset of the reforms, most young people wanted to go to the US more than anywhere else, they all had an American Dream. In Meng Xiaojun's eyes, 'the so-called American Dream is that everyone has an equal chance to fulfil their dreams; only in the US can you do this'. At the start of the film, the three central characters go to the US embassy separately to process their visa applications. Cheng Dongqing's application is rejected, Wang Dan gives up his visa, and only Meng Xiaojun's application is successful. The narrator, Cheng Dongqing, says in an aside, 'he would not be able to imagine that twenty years later, the thing he would be best at would be helping other people to go to the US'. The greatest irony is that someone who was refused a visa to the US many times, a loser who had never been to the US, should become the king of overseas study. The New Dream tuition school he sets up attains success precisely through tutoring English and peddling the American Dream. New Dream's core competitive strength is peddling the dream, sending more and more students to the US to study. For the three central characters, the American Dream of going to the US had been shattered, but when New Dream becomes successful in China, New Dream becomes the protagonists' China Dream. The English-language title *American Dream in China* summarised this central theme very accurately. The process of the realisation of the China Dream not only involves seeking material wealth, but also winning recognition from people for your aspirations.

The contrasting of a constantly changing, ever more successful China Dream with a conservative, naïve, blindly self-aggrandising American Dream is satisfying. The feeling of success gives the film an emotional payoff. Wang Dan's girlfriend is depicted as a sexually liberated American girl who sees love as a kind of baggage. The US visa official is the image of coldness and inflexibility, the American waitress in the restaurant short changes poor Chinese students, the American professor in the laboratory is heartless and, on top of all that, the representative of the 'EES', the film's fictional US education oversight body, is domineering and wholly lacking respect for others. In summary, the film depicts Americans as not understanding how people work, lacking awareness of the rest of the world, and blind to the huge changes in China; obstinate, prejudiced, inflexible, and unfriendly, especially to Chinese people. Yet even though the film in effect wants to tell the audience that the American Dream has been shattered and the Chinese Dream has been realised, the success of the protagonists depends on peddling the American Dream. They also aspire to achieving American approval of their success, to be marked by the listing of their company on the US stock markets. Their success is still an American Dream. This obviously oversimplifies the rich and varied implications of the spirit of the age of reform and opening up, and thus the values expressed in this film are full of contradictions.[11]

BEYOND THE CHINA DREAM AND THE AMERICAN DREAM

Zhongguo Hehuoren, at the same time as being a high box office success and getting broad praise from the general public, encountered fierce criticism from many intellectuals and public figures in the cultural sphere. The sharpest criticism was directed at the values being transmitted in the film as acceptable.[12] According to *Labour Daily* (*Laodong Bao*), the audience's enthusiastic praise of *Zhongguo Hehuoren* should have let the director Peter Chan sit back and relax, but following the good reception of the film, reviews from all sides expressed negative opinions. One argument was that the film was advocating 'money is everything' values. Xia Shang wrote on Weibo, '*Zhongguo Hehuoren* is full of Chinese-style models of success. The end tribute shots made you feel like vomiting; it is a typically philistine, mercenary film.'[13] The producers abandoned screenings in Hong Kong and Macau, assuming that the film would not be well received on the international market and would suffer at the box office; there was no way the values it expressed would gain international approval. The film was tailor made for the domestic Chinese market. In the last forty years China has undergone enormous changes. Almost overnight there was a transformation from an agricultural to an industrial society. People exclaim in admiration how China, in only forty years, has gone through a journey that took the West three hundred years. However, China's value systems and spiritual orientation have yet to complete the same leap from tradition to modernity. Right up to the present, a core value system for Chinese society has still not been established. When the great material success of the China Dream is praised, we need also to consider the spiritual and emotional implications of the change. Considering the future from today's standpoint, we need to explore new values structures and spiritual directions.

Many analysts hold that the film tells the story of a hypocritical striving for success, using the demagogic practice of success to whitewash reality, and stupefy the audience.[14] There are many scenes in the film showing the central characters glowing with self-satisfaction after making large amounts of money. When Cheng Dongqing makes a lot of money for the first time and gives half of it to Wang Yang, Wang shouts out 'We're rich', throws the money into the air, and that evening goes to a karaoke bar to drink and look for pretty girls. Through his screaming and shouting in the karaoke bar he is giving vent to the emotions of sudden success after many years of failure. His immediate and wild recklessness has the image of a typical get-rich-quick type. The second time, after New Dream has achieved even greater success, being transformed into a public company and making a huge profit, Cheng Dongqing first puts money into a cloth bag, then into a safe. Cheng, Meng, and Wang smoke big cigars as they survey the piles of money; their faces bear the expression of success. The third time, when New Dream has been listed on the US stock market, they go to Las Vegas, where Cheng loses a serious amount of money. For the film to portray this kind of China Dream to the Chinese public is irresponsible. In effect it says that it doesn't matter whether or not you have failed in the past, so long as your success means you can live in a Western-style mansion, drive a big car, drink Lafitte '82 and gamble for high stakes. This kind of high achiever is, on the one hand, worshipped by the masses but, on the other hand, treats money like dirt. The film shows a simplistic understanding of success as the achievement of wealth. This is a shallow understanding of the earlier period of the American Dream, as well as dealing with the China Dream in an oversimplified way. Many critics regard the film as 'setting up memorials and writing hagiographies' of high achievers, showing only the glorious aspect of the unfolding of the China Dream but hiding the ugly aspects of how wealth is gained.

The Chinese-style partnership type of success presented in the film is in fact the normal experience of many Chinese in the past forty years. But we must also understand that this type of success is the product of a society undergoing exceptional changes and should lead the audience to consider a new kind of life value. What the China Dream conveys to some is that you are either a success with immense wealth or you are a loser trodden under by other people, leading a lowly, ant-like existence. The China Dream must not only represent wealth, but it should represent stability, a kindly relationship between people, cultural freedom and acceptance; it should represent how every person, through honest work and wisdom, can lead a life worthy of respect. And this would of course include recognition and respect for the value of small business. Works of art in the current period should reject preaching the obsolete idea that 'if you succeed you are a king; if you fail you are a bandit'. They should be conveying the message that in this 'world of dust', our mortal life, amongst normal, unsuccessful people there are values that surpass success. Society must become more humane and caring towards ordinary people, and reveal the nobility and beauty there is in mortal existence. The humanity of ordinary individuals should gain them the respect of others – as exactly when, at the end of the film, Cheng Dongqing and his former girlfriend Sumei meet again, he had hoped she would compliment him on his success and say something like 'I feel proud of how successful you are today'. He had not imagined that Sumei would not even mention his success but take a contrary position, saying, 'the important thing is not success, but in being a normal person, you cannot forfeit your dignity'. She reminds us that dignity is more important than success, whether in the context of the American Dream or the Chinese Dream. The director is reminding us that we need to make a profound examination (and self-examination) of the spiritual and moral crises that face contemporary China. The film shows that in today's China, although individual economic status is gradually rising, we are still a long way from completely shaking off the influence of the 'American Dream', and we are still a long way from finally extricating ourselves from the habit of taking the West as the reference point for self-approval.

As to the rise of China's aspiration for international approval, the method provided by the film is still the vengeful style of anti-colonialism; that is, films such as *Huo Yuan Jia* (Fearless, 2006), *Ye Wen* (Ip Man, 2008), *Huang Fei Hong* (Once Upon a Time in China, 1991), in which China's people become strong, fully awakened, and have a great battle with the Western colonialists, defeating them. This offers the satisfaction of an image of revenge. In *Zhongguo Hehuoren* the highpoint of the story is when the three lead characters go to the US to negotiate with representatives of the EES over piracy and copyright infringement. Meng Xiaojun takes Cheng Dongqing and Wang Yang for a meal in the restaurant where he had once worked, and tells them about his failures and the racism he had encountered in the US. This is the second time he has brought New Dream to the US for negotiations, but the Americans show no respect at all – at the airport his luggage is searched repeatedly, an American company representative he had an appointment with stands him up and refuses to see him. This makes him realise that only when New Dream has been listed on the New York Stock Exchange will they gain the respect and acknowledgement of Americans. Cheng Dongqing says, 'let's go and have dinner, and storm the US', and they smile with satisfaction at each other. And so, when they are negotiating with the EES, each expresses their personal agency. First, Wang Yang deliberately behaves badly, disregarding etiquette and regulations. In the middle of the negotiations, he goes to the toilet, and insults the US representatives. Then Cheng Dongqing, seeing that the US side are not giving any ground, turns the tables by casually acknowledging they have pirated and infringed on copyright, and he skilfully turns the US representative's accusations into their having doubts about Chinese students' ability to do exams. Cheng blows this out of proportion, and puts his own ideas across with vehemence: 'We don't like being called thieves, we know where we have made mistakes, but you don't know your mistakes, and you don't care about that. China is changing, it is regrettable that you have not changed. China is the world's largest market for English, Chinese students don't come to the US to stay here, they want to go back home.' His highly emotional speech criticises Americans' stubborn adherence to their own opinions, and their lack of understanding of the changes in China. After that, he says, with the huge China market as the enticement, that New China is open to cooperation, leaving the US representative struck dumb. The Chinese audience takes a vicarious part in the battle: they see Uncle Sam being defeated in Manhattan by Chinese people, delighting in feelings of the self-respect, national respect, and self-aggrandisement won by a small businessperson, and set to the resounding tones of 'The Internationale'; New Dream, an obvious copyright infringer and lawbreaker, becomes a national hero conquering for the glory of the nation: as Cheng Dongqing puts it at the outset of the film, '[let's] plant our red flags all over America.'[15]

In recent years, such films promoting nationalist emotions have been successful with Chinese audiences. For example, *Wolf Warrior 2* (2017), directed by and starring Wu Jing, had the highest box office takings in China, in large part by peddling nationalism (to an even greater extent than *Zhongguo Hehuoren*). Using nationalism as a value for the purposes of promotion excites popular feelings and unites the masses, but at the same time there is a huge risk. Nationalism is a double-edged sword; while it has the positive use of bringing together the people, at the same time it can be used arrogantly and foster prejudice. Towards the end of *Zhongguo Hehuoren*, when the three main characters leave the concluded negotiations, they drive crazily around New York in their luxury car and give vent to the excitement of victory after long-suppressed feelings of failure. Wang Yang says 'we've got them by the balls' and momentarily lets go of the steering wheel while Meng Xiaojun flashes a middle finger. These inelegant expressions of disdain for the US reveal an unprecedented and incomparable feeling of pride in oneself and cultural conceit brought on by success. This is not beneficial to China's image, or to the exporting of China's culture.[16] China is a large country increasing in power and overemphasised nationalism will make other countries feel that it is a threat. Even looking at it internally, emphasising nationalism also might cause conflict among China's different minority nationalities.

The China Dream must not perpetuate the limited thought process of failure versus vengeance: 'If you are backward, you will take a beating.' This kind of tragic national feeling played a part in China's rapid development in the twentieth century, but in the globalised era of today, it is out of place. Nationalism in the past had an intrinsic fairness, but over-inflated nationalism can develop into imperialism. In the current era, the China Dream should broadcast kindliness and tolerance, the image of an open and peaceful country, contributing to the world a new orientation of values and emotions.

Today, multiculturalism is mainstream across the world. Neither China nor the US is a homogenous 'other', and both need to reflect on the coloniser's value systems that emphasis strength over weakness. The contemporary China Dream needs a new worldview, a new value system, and a new emotional perspective. The China Dream for the future needs to have a new imagination, one that reflects China's experiences of the last two hundred years but recognises a very much changed world and is willing to consider new possibilities, and from here, unfold the creation of a new politico-economic order.[17] In the past it was exactly because of excessive emphasis on wounds inflicted in our history that we were inhibited from applying a more moderate and inclusive mentality to understanding our condition and to constructing a dream of the future that is truly our own. As China becomes ever more powerful, we must remain conscious that individual and national respect are not gained entirely through the power of money; we must contribute new wisdom and expound new social values to win respect.

NOTES

1. Zhang Zuqun, 'Dianyin "Zhongguo Meng" de Zhengzhixing Shuxie: Yi *Zhongguo Hehuoren* wei Lie' [Film(s) of the "China Dream" political writings: taking *Zhongguo Hehuoren* as an example], *Dianying Pinglun* 19 (2013): 7–10; Bao Xueqian, 'Hua Hu Bucheng Fanleigou – Xianhua Dianying *Zhongguo Hehuoren*' [You can't make a dog into a tiger just by painting it – discussing *Zhongguo Hehuoren*], *Hong Dou* 8 (2013): 79–82; Wang Jue, 'Zhongguo Ren de Meiguo Meng' [The Chinese people's American Dream], *Shehui Guancha* 7 (2013): 88–90.
2. Xi Jinping's speech at the *Road to Revitalisation* exhibition, 29 November 2012, reproduced in *People's Daily*, 30 November 2012.
3. Zhang Yi, 'Chen Kexing Bo Yu Minyong: *Hehuoren* bushi Dongfang Zhuanjipian' [Peter Chan refutes Yu Minhong: *Zhongguo Hehuoren* is not a biopic of New Orient], *Zhongguo Xinwenwang*, 23 May 2013.

4. Zhan Muxun [Frederic Jameson], *Wanqi Zibenzhuyi Wenhua Luoji* [The logic of late-capitalist culture] (Beijing: Sanlian Shudian, 1997), 523.
5. Zhang Yanguo, '"Zhongguo Jueqi" de Minzu Yuyan: Dianying Zhongguo Hehuoren de Yishi Xintai Jiangou Celüe [The national fable of 'China's rise to prominence' – the tactical framework of the ideology of the film *Zhongguo Hehuoren*], Dianying Wenxue 24 (2013): 79–80.
6. Xi Jinping's speech at the *Road to Revitalisation* exhibition, 29 November 2012.
7. Zhan Muxun [Frederic Jameson], *Wanqi Zibenzhuyi Wenhua Luoji*, 544.
8 Xi Jinping's speech at the *Road to Revitalisation* exhibition, 29 November 2012.
9. Pan Wei, Ma Ya, eds, *Jujie Dangdai Zhongguo Jiazhi Guan* [Focus on current Chinese values] (Beijing: Sanlian shudian, 2008), 198.
10. This is a witty joke and impossible to translate: jumping into the ocean means leaving the protection of state, like putting dumplings into boiling water to cook them.
11. Wang Yichuan, 'Shidai Jingshen de Chouli yu Bianxing – Cong Zhongguo Hehuoren Kan Gaige shidai de Wenhua Jiazhi Jiangou [Distortion and disengagement from the spirit of the age – *Zhonguo Hehuoren* and the spiritual structure of the era of reform and opening up], *Dangdai Dianying* 7 (2013): 28–40.
12. *Zhonguo Hehuoren* has been caricatured as expressing 'three incorrect values' (*san guan buzheng*) in a discussion on the Baidu message boards, see http://tieba.baidu.com/p/2358559111.
13. *Dalian Wanbao*, 28 May 2013.
14. As above, see http://tieba.baidu.com/p/2358559111.
15. Tian Huiqun, '*Zhongguo Hehuoren*: Chuantong/Xiandai? Dongfang/Xifang?' [*Zhongguo Hehuoren*: Traditional or Modern? East or West?], *Dangdai Dianying* 42 (2013): 40–42.
16. Song Fagang, 'Guozu Rentong Beihou Wenhua Ziye – *Zhongguo Hehuoren* de Jiazhi Biaoda yu Xiuci Liehen' [Cultural conceit behind nation and race identification/approval – values expressed in *Zhonguo Hehuoren* and cracks in the rhetoric], *Guancha yu Piping* 24 (2013): 4–5.
17. Zhang Huiyu et al., 'Dangdai Dazhong Wenhua Zhong de Meiguo Xiangxiang' [American imagination in contemporary mass culture], *Wenyi Lilun yu Piping* 5 (2013): 43–52.

6

Between Reality and Utopia: Chinese Underclass Literature since the 1990s

Jiaona Xu

Since the 1990s, literature and films have appeared that reflect the life of the underclasses of society in a period of transformation. They pay particular attention to the predicament of disadvantaged groups living at a subsistence level, including peasant workers, impoverished peasants, and the urban poor. These amply illustrate the spirit of humanist care and the realism of contemporary writers. However, in the majority of cases their descriptions of the space in which the underclass subsist are based on a simple binary opposition – city versus countryside, modern versus traditional, good versus bad. Through a kind of de-historicising and de-politicising, they compose a very moving elegy for a lost countryside, the lost village, and lost traditional values. They respond to the identity crisis and spiritual predicament of the underclasses with the ache of nostalgia, but without helping to form an accurate understanding of history and actuality.

Since the 'new age',[1] there has been a deepening transformation of society – the comprehensive unfolding of reform and opening up. The structural readjustments and shifting circumstances have promoted the rapid economic development of society, and at the same time have been a divisive force; they have created a fissure between a section of society and the main socioeconomic system,[2] which has resulted in the formation of an increasingly massive underclass, a world made up of a disadvantaged community of peasant workers, impoverished peasants, and urban poor. 'The features encapsulated by this concept "underclass" are more than what concepts like disadvantage, marginalisation, inferiority can express . . . underclass refers to the community which has been rejected by the system, meaning they are being split away from the mainstream of economic social organisation.'[3] Against this backdrop, since the 1990s, there has come to the fore a batch of literary, artistic, and visual works that reflect the life circumstances of the underclass in this time of transition, paying close attention to the predicament of the disadvantaged community in its pursuit of survival. These works have produced heated debate among the critics. The principal subjects of these underclass narratives are peasant workers coming to urban areas from the countryside; they unavoidably deal with the city and the farming villages, and with the place where city and countryside meet: the city/countryside 'fracture zone'. This chapter, using selected representative works, analyses how underclass literature and art constructs the experiences and imagination of the underclass population. It reveals their emotional structure and spiritual crisis and examines the forms that the utopian impulse takes in the context of the hard lives of the underclass.

CITY AND COUNTRYSIDE: BINARY SPACE

The antagonism between city and countryside has been the core problem of China's modernisation over the last one hundred years, but has differed at different stages in its nature and in the way it has been manifested. In the new era, with the powerful development of market economics, the difference in economic structures and incomes between city and country has encouraged excess labour to flow from the countryside towards the cities, to flow from the underdeveloped west of the country to the coastal areas in the east, thus creating a characteristically Chinese tide of migrant labour. Throughout this process, on the one hand is the accelerating disintegration of traditional agricultural society and the rural culture that it nurtures – the countryside day by day declining and becoming more depressed, problems piling on top of one another. On the other hand, because of the limitations set by the household registration (*hukou*) system, there is no way for the peasants who arrive in the cities to be truly accepted, or enjoy equal material, medical, cultural, or educational resources. The acute antagonism between city and country has become the background for almost all the underclass literature of the new century. Against this background, the underclass live, experience, dream, and ponder. Peasant labourers wander between city and countryside: 'going to the city' and 'returning to the countryside' have formed the two most important themes in underclass literature since the turn of the century. In these works, city and countryside are not only the material space where they live, but even more a reflection of the world of their psychology and consciousness, and because of this they get tangled up in contradictions, forming complicated relationships.

Compared to the poor and weak countryside, in the city there are plentiful material goods, numerous opportunities, and cultured and developed lifestyles. The city is the way out for the desperate, impoverished peasant to make a living in Chen Yingsong's *A Dog Called Taiping*; it is the 'bright light' to the eyes of the peasant in Li Peifu's *City Light*; and it symbolises the 'good prospects' which are the heart's desire of generation after generation in Cao Duoyong's *Good Prospects in the City*. But the bright side of the city exists only in the imagination of migrant workers, in their 'city dreams'. When they get to the city, they engage in the dirtiest, hardest work, without any safeguards; they suffer prejudice and exploitation from every side, living in odious and cramped rented accommodation. Destitute and homeless, their city dreams, in the end, in the face of cruel reality, will come to nothing.

The famous writer Jia Pingwa wrote many works reflecting the fortunes and sufferings of the countryside and the peasants in this era of transformation. His long novel *Gaoxing* (Happy) portrayed the peasants Liu Gaoxing (Happy Liu) and Wufu coming into the city and eking out a hard living as ragpickers. Liu Gaoxing, the central character, yearns for and approves of the city. In his eyes, the city represents culture, elegance, beauty, and fashion. And not only that, he makes a conscious effort to become a city person and in his lifestyle he positively engages with the city. He likes to be neat and tidy, follows the rules and always offers to help other people. When he meets with prejudice, he doesn't stubbornly protest, but reflects it back on himself: 'When she treats me with indifference, it must be that she sees nothing in me worthy of respect.'[4] But after arriving in the city the only way Gaoxing and Wufu can make a living is rubbish picking. They live in an unfinished and abandoned building in a village within the city, picking up green leaves left behind in the vegetable market and bringing them home to eat, enduring the discrimination of city dwellers. To earn more money, they go to the large rubbish dump outside the city in the early evening to pick rubbish; halfway through the night, they go to the labour market and get work unloading cement. In the end they are conned by a 'blackhearted' boss into going to dig sewers. Eventually, Wufu dies in a state of desperate poverty. The city is indifferent and unfeeling; the little person from the underclass is swallowed up and destroyed.

In such writings about the city, the ultimate point is the internal contradictions and sufferings of the underclass, revealing their identity crises and lack of meaningful values. Seeking a better life, following the progress of urbanisation, they come flooding into the cities, filled with dreams and restlessness. When faced with cruel reality, they discover that they are in, but do not belong to, the city; there is no place for them. They float around in the city, yearning to be part of it but remaining alien. They are drawn in involuntarily, but again pushed aside. Love and hatred of the city occur simultaneously. The rootless life of this underclass is completely different in nature from that in Kerouac's *On the Road*, despite their shared transience. Their actions cannot be seen as critical of culture or society. Also, they are different from the intellectuals of the May Fourth period, who were deeply attached to the beauty of the countryside and, from a rational viewpoint, consciously criticised and rejected the city because of the negative influence of industrial culture. The hostility to the city of the underclass is much more based on an estranged and polarised relationship; it is a passive, compelled, see-saw battle.

The people drifting around in the city yearn for a home; for this reason, memories of their old home always have a utopian complexion. In *Gaoxing*, when it is the season for the harvest Gaoxing and Wufu have no chance to go back to their village. Gaoxing recalls the scenes of harvesting the grain in their village: 'I have smelled the ripe grain, smelled the ladybugs crawling all over the sheaves of wheat and the moths, smelled the odour coming off the bodies of the harvesters, these smells are fragrant, but they're also sour and stinking, all blended together at dusk, curling and swirling like a fog, spreading through the lanes of the village.'[5] This recollection expresses the pure and profound feelings that peasants have for the soil, but another aspect is that the recollection has filtered out the poor and humble, vulgar and coarse, filtered out the hardship and monotony of agricultural work, and turned it poetic.

The old home is the roots for the wanderer from home; therefore, the final outcome of the 'going to the city' narrative is the return home. The final outcome in *Gaoxing* is the tragic death of Wufu, with Liu Gaoxing journeying for hundreds of miles carrying the corpse back to the village. *A Dog Called Taiping* by Chen Yingsong, a novella written from a dog's point of view, describes Cheng Dazhong, a peasant from Shen Nong Jia (in Hubei province), coming to the city and seeking shelter with his paternal aunt. After being chased out of that home, all he can do is sleep under the arches of a bridge, with tramps and beggars as companions; ultimately dying in a toxic factory. Watching helplessly as his master dies an unnatural death, Cheng's faithful and true mountain dog, by the skin of its teeth, makes it back home.[6] In the short novel *Shoulder Pole* by Li Rui, the carpenter Jin Tang, who has lost both legs, using a shoulder pole and car tyres, with his two hands, push by push, gets himself back home. When he sees the old spirit tree at the entrance to his village, 'his tears suddenly flooded down like a torrent of rain'.[7] In underclass literature the theme of returning home is replayed over and over again with great clamour. After the high tide of emotion has passed, what remains is still a powerless feeling of a predicament that is difficult to resolve: it is exactly because of the economic insecurity of making a living in the countryside that people are forced to leave their native place; so, when they come home, what next?

In this sense, the theme of returning home deconstructs the nostalgic utopia established by the 'going to the city' narrative. In reality, the dilapidation and darkness of the rural village is truly shocking. The novella *Our Road* by Luo Weizhang narrates in the first person the story of how the protagonist manages to get the only remaining train ticket home before Chinese New Year, and gives it to Chun Mei, a girl from his village. In the end he abandons a fee being held by his boss and determinedly returns home to see his wife and daughter whom he hasn't seen for five years. But when he reaches home, life is still poverty stricken, and there is no living to be made. In addition, witnessing in person how the villagers mock and gang up on Chun Mei, who had been deceived and had a child before marriage, fills him with discouragement and depression, and, finally bidding farewell to his wife and daughter, he sets off for the city again. The novella touches on nearly all the ailments of the contemporary countryside, such as problems of ignorant conservatism, the loss of the young, strong workforce, farmland going to waste, hollowed-out villages, children left behind, etc. In this way, for underclass people 'returning to one's old home is like arriving in a strange land';[8] they can only go back and forth indecisively between the city and the countryside, with nowhere to rest.

Modern spatial theory tells us that space is absolutely not simply something that exists in the objective sense of physics, but exists multi-dimensionally in social culture and territory, just as Lefebvre has said: 'space is pervaded by social relationships, it is not only supported by social relationships, it produces and is produced by social relationships'.[9] Put another way, space defines subjectivity, just as the French poet Noel Arnaud has said, 'I am the space where I am.'[10] But when addressing those people who have left the land, and are drifting in the cities, they are neither marginal, nor are they outsiders, they are people without a position and, possessing no space whatsoever, they are the sector that 'has been shoved aside by the structure'. In these circumstances in which they are being pulled back and forth from the countryside to the city, by what means are the underclass to consolidate their sense of self? They are coerced and pressed to the point of shattering. China's country–city fault zones, compared with the slums in Western society, reflect not only economic and social conflicts, but also identity anxiety and crisis.

Given these conditions, underclass literature's descriptions, concerning another type of space intimately connected to people's existence – their private space – deserves particular attention. Xia Tianmin, a writer from Yunnan province, wrote a short novel called *Kissing on Chang'an Avenue*; it relates the emotional experiences of a pair of lovers, Xiao Jiang and Liu Cui, who come from a distant mountain area of Yunnan to work in Beijing, 'the heart of the motherland'. Their love story looks romantic but is embarrassing and awkward. In the bustling capital city Xiao Jiang develops a strong urge to share a kiss with his lover on Chang'an Avenue. He is himself deeply humble, and he would attempt through this unusual act to diminish his distance from city people, gaining a feeling of identity recognition: 'at least in spirit, I am in accord with these city people'.[11] He meets with failure twice. The first time because he has not communicated his intention to Liu Cui in advance; misunderstood as playing the hooligan, Liu Cui boxes his ears on the street, after which he is beaten by passersby. The second time, even though he had got Liu Cui's approval and has planned it carefully, a motorcade of foreign official visitors is passing through; Chang'an Avenue is sealed off and the plan comes to nothing. Eventually, however, his wish is realised with the encouragement and help of his colleagues, and Xiao Jiang and Liu Cui 'kissed naturally, kissed vigorously, kissed without inhibition, and with surging passion'.[12] This act has become a performance, a declaration, a concrete objectification of the unconscious, a manifestation of the desire and will of the group.

For the time being, let's not say whether the beauty and meaning of this scene was wishful imagination of the author, the fact that it puts what originally ought to be the private secret of love and sex together with Chang'an Avenue and Tian'anmen Rostrum with all their political connotations, ceding the private space to the grand narrative, makes even more distinct the embarrassing position of underclass self-perception. In many more instances, the private space is absent in underclass creative works; images and notions of 'home' are basically in a state of concealment. Yet this kind of emptiness authentically reflects the life situation of underclass people. They abandon their wives (or husbands) and children, coming alone to seek a living in the city, squashed into dilapidated and overcrowded cheap rental accommodation, with no fixed abode, in a precarious state. But the fact that this concept has been forgotten also reveals another aspect of their spiritual state. Because life is so hard and they have given up holding on to their notion of home, at this time of the approach of huge crisis of the spirit, it is also very hard to find meanings and values that can act as supporting pillars. The absence of a home has resulted in unravelling of ethical standards and a value vacuum. The novel *Mother* by Chen Yingsong tells the story of five children who cannot bear their heavy responsibility, and in the end conspire to hound to death their chronically ill and bed-bound mother – this is really shocking.[13] Perhaps this tragedy has been created by society, we are powerless, but it is always the bottom line of the humanity and ethics that is interrogated.

THE SENSE OF BEING ADRIFT AND NOSTALGIA

The city and countryside described in the underclass literature of the new era is not only the actual space the underclass live in, it also is the carrier of their personal experiences and their imagination, and has represented the emotional structure of being adrift. But this is not the only thing; they are also objects of intellectual writers' projection of feelings and psychology; that is, underclass people's displacement is overlaid with the drifting feeling of the intellectual. The heavy nostalgia enveloping these works on many occasions is the intervention of the writer.

Many underclass works use the voice of the author to tell the story, the intellectual acting as the narrator in the first person, with their personal feelings thrown right into the work. One example is another famous underclass work, the novella *The Ballad of the Sister-in-Law* by Luo Weizhang, winner of the tenth Ba Jin Literary Award. It takes an intellectual who goes from the country to the city as the 'I', absorbed into the life of his fifty-three-year-old sister-in-law who has been forced to make a living and go out to work. Narrated in a highly emotional style, it is a tragic, heroic, and moving story. Even in those works which are narrated from the viewpoint of the underclass person, the main character is often changed by the subjective consciousness of the writer. The narrator of *Our Road* is a peasant, who goes to the city to sell his labour, but he has been educated, he is a person of culture, rare in villages. The character of Gaoxing in *Gaoxing*, even though he is underclass by birth, has white skin and plays the flute beautifully. This type of character construct is reasonable in itself, after all it's their having received a certain amount of education that enables them to take on the function of the narrator and produce such responses and thoughts. However, it also reflects the writers' preference for telling rather than depicting the lives and stories of the underclass; no matter if it is the images of the characters or the conflicts of the story, it is all presented in terms of concepts, metaphors, and elaborated emotions. Another aspect is that the writer is unable to adhere to the standpoint of cold reason, but allows his own subjectivity and limited vision to interfere with the balanced development of the story. In this way it is easy to slide into binary frameworks, to impose a simplification of the relationship of city and countryside, modern and traditional, good and bad, etc., and this means that, when faced with the predicaments and hardships of the underclass, there is no way the writer can carry out an in-depth and intense examination. Thus, the works become suffused with a distinct feeling that this is just the way it is, even to the extent of making emotional states of self-pity and narcissism seem inescapable.

Many of the authors who write underclass literature came out of the villages themselves; and even though they have entered the system, with a steady income and reputation, and have lived in the city for many years, they still can't accept the city and even hold onto strong feelings of enmity. In the epilogue to *Gaoxing*, Jia Pingwa frankly admits, 'I was surprised to discover that, even though I have lived in the city for several decades, and ordinarily boast of having a modern consciousness, I still have a bad case of peasant consciousness, and in the depths of my heart, abhor the city, hate the city, and in my works I am disgusted with the city, hate the city on behalf of those ragged people I write about.'[14] Chen Yingsong also confesses freely, 'I dislike the city, rich people, films and novels with magnificent houses. I think that all of their acting is affected. Their suffering is extremely unreal, their neuroses, their perversions, make me sick. It's only the feelings of peasants and little people which are realistic, their sufferings are incomparably fine, and their happiness brings out the tears.'[15] As a result they start out from the subjective negativist viewpoint, they give a dark complexion to, even demonise, the city. In *Gaoxing* all of the city people are selfish, ruthless, and unfeeling; in *A Dog Called Taiping* even the city dogs are steeped in evil and worthy of damnation.

Maligning the city is a continuous theme within China's literature of the last hundred years. In this can be seen the culture of traditional Confucian ethics, the respect for agriculture and care for the rural and the belittling of commercial thinking, and its influence on writers. But today's reality is already very different from the 1920s and 1930s. Early modernisation in China was passive, and was tied in with the national memory of humiliation, but since reform and opening up, modernisation has become an eager choice actively made by the entire population; there is nothing that can stop the progress of urbanisation. With the widening of the gap between town and country, the countryside is even more destitute and dark; the poetic rural village ceased to exist some time ago. The peasant is day by day becoming more estranged from the soil, particularly with the new generation of peasant workers of the 1980s and 1990s who do not possess the kind of deep feelings for the land of their father's generation. Their feelings of identity with the countryside are also gradually weakening, and the city has a greater attraction for them. The crime of those who write underclass literature is that when they are describing the city, not only have they no choice but to face up to the fact that it is fair and just for the peasants to seek a better life coming into the towns, but when they are dealing with the contradictions between the two and they are arranging the fortunes and the ways forward for their characters, they frequently expose a sense of being powerless and helpless.

In the current period of transition, faced with the complexity of China's modernity, many people are unable to gain a foothold in the flood of history, unable to grasp national, racial, collective, even individual circumstances and future prospects; the feeling of drifting has become the normal symptom of the age. It is exactly in this sense, that we can understand why nostalgic culture can pervade and thrive in China right now and nostalgia has become a normal structure of feeling.

Nostalgia is a traditional subject in literature; it is the repository of cherished memories and strong attachment to the home village for the traveller wandering aimlessly in strange lands. But nostalgia inseparably combined with modernity is in essence a feeling without foundation; it is a reliance on a utopian home that no longer exists. From serious literature and art films to mass culture, we can see all different types of nostalgia texts. The medium for this nostalgia can be in terms of timeliness, for example the loss of youth, such as Vicki Zhao's maiden film *So Young* (2013) to the film *Fang Hua* (2017) by

Feng Xiaogang (see Chapter 4), which sparked off heated comments. It can be in terms of location, for example the countryside in 'returning home' writings; it can be in terms of the endangered traditional society, for example *The Song of the Phoenix* (2016) directed by Wu Tianming, is a dirge played on the suona (a traditional Chinese double-reeded horn), an elegy for the decline of the traditional art that the suona itself represents. It can even be in terms of the earth itself, for example the film which has been called the inception point of China's first year of science fiction, *The Wandering Earth* (2019). The objects of appeal in all of these are things which have become beautiful because they have already been, or are about to be, lost; in the process of recollection or yearning for the past they have been disengaged from their complex historical context, stripped of their serious political colour, crystallised, purified into value symbols, and wrapped up in abundant, richly sentimental hues.

In the current, immense process of modernisation, the elimination of rural China is accelerating, the relationship between the people and land and labour is becoming increasingly distant, traditional values are disintegrating, people don't have the time to bid a proper farewell to the past. All kinds of new values hit you in the face, causing people to be suddenly caught unawares by emotions of rootless drifting. Compared with the feelings of being adrift and of anxiety that arise with modernity, nostalgia looks superficial and pallid, a very unreliable strategy. It always converges unavoidably with pessimistic emotions, Individuals knowingly or unwittingly become vaguely aware of a reality they are unable to grasp. They perceive their own limitations in the face of the uncertainty of the present and the unpredictability of the future. Yet they still retain the impulse and ability to imagine a more beautiful life.

So far as underclass literature is concerned, the ideological function of nostalgia is even more obvious. Using the pain of nostalgia to respond to the identity crisis and spiritual predicament of the underclass is not only unhelpful in creating an accurate understanding and profound grasp of history and reality; it also cannot provide a good answer to the problem of the way forward for the underclass. The vehicle for nostalgia is located in tradition, countryside, the past; it is always internalising a sort of alternative perspective. Since the May

Fourth and New Culture movements, in rural literature works there often exists a double stereotype: either it is acting out the countryside as a beautiful Garden of Eden, seeing it as the deliverance from the degenerate modern city; or it is understanding it as an ossified and constraining feudal prison, providing the drilling ground of the Enlightenment. No matter which attitude it takes, at the root of it, they are all a kind of binary opposite imagination of 'otherness'. The existence of the underclass must in itself form a criticism and satire of the modernisation model, inspiring an imagination for and consideration of another possible modernity. But when the bulk of underclass literature portrays with care and effort the distinctiveness of this class of person, and justifies the underclass as the modern 'heterogenous space', that makes it into a tool of modern ideology. Even more scary, by accident or design, is that we are all 'consumers of the underclass', i.e., using it to maintain our rather fragile sense of superiority and sense of safety.

If we had an integrated vision of the course of China's modernisation, we would see in the transformation period at the end of the twentieth century that the relationship between urban and rural China was extremely complex. The city was not entirely the den of iniquity, nor was the countryside the poetic pastoral. City and country have never been independent, or separable. Many of the problems of the countryside have been caused by the city: the development of the countryside, frequently, has been duplicating – 'copycatting' – the city. The problems which modernisation has brought to cities are bound together with the problems left behind by tradition, making the problems in the countryside even more complex and serious. If writers of underclass literature want to produce works with depth, they must have a view of historical development and a 'multi-critical' vision, engaging with complex, difficult revelations and meditations, and work hard to get a grip on the confusing and complicated, but fundamental, things behind the social reality.

CONSTRUCTING AESTHETIC UTOPIA

In underclass literature we see underclass people wandering in the margin between city and country, not occupying a stable space, burdened with identity anxieties. However, in this process of modernisation, the sensation of drifting fits with the structures of feeling of the majority of people, and together they form the spiritual malaise of the period of transformation. What decides the achievements and limits of underclass literature is certainly not its exceptional subject matter but the same problem as that faced by China's contemporary literature in general: how will writers create, for the mass of common people being dragged forward in the surging flood of historical change, an aesthetic sense that can bring coherence to their lives?

In this regard, the young director Bi Gan's maiden film, *Kaili Blues* (2016), which had a stunning effect on the world of cinema, is a rare paragon, and can give much inspiration to current underclass writing. The film is set in the damp, peaceful subtropical landscape of Bi Gan's old home in southeast Guizhou province. The main character, Chen Sheng, is a doctor, living an empty life in a rundown clinic in the suburbs of the county town of Kaili. When he was young he had spent some time in the underworld. With his wife falling ill, he accepts financial assistance from the underworld boss Hua Heshang, and later, as an act of comradeship, takes revenge on Hua Heshang's enemy, which results in his committing a crime for which he spends nine years in prison. By the time he gets out, his mother and wife have both died of illness. He is filled with remorse and frustration, living as if in a permanent nightmare, and deeply estranged from his younger brother, Laowai. Only his little nephew Weiwei can give a sliver of spiritual sustenance and consolation. Later, Weiwei is sold by Laowai to Hua Heshang; Chen Sheng goes to seek him out. When he reaches the town of Dangmai, he unexpectedly runs into a young person also called Weiwei who is kind, generous, and in brave pursuit of love. Chen Sheng also meets a woman who looks just like his ex-wife who owns a hairdressing salon. He asks her to cut his hair, tells her his story, and sings an out-of-tune nursery rhyme to her in the square of the village, completing his soul's redemption. In the end, when he reaches the town of Zhenyuan and sees that little Weiwei is leading a happy and carefree life under the care of Hua Heshang, he decides to let him go and be brought up by Hua Heshang, who himself had suffered the painful loss of his own child.

The film establishes Kaili, Dangmai, and Zhenyuan as three geographic spaces, all equally realistic; but Dangmai is also a magical realm filled with poetical meaning. While describing the real life of Kaili, the film, through montage editing, brings in reality, recollection, nightmare, hallucination, and the sounds of different kinds of bothersome people. On the level of meaning, it adopts a shattering effect to reflect the way in which Cheng Sheng's real world is being cut up by his past. And, in contrast to this, through a single forty-two-minute shot, the film narrates the story of what happens in Dangmai. By the method of keeping as close as possible to reality, the film creates a place of dreams, or you could say, an aesthetic utopia. The continuous circulating movement of the camera creates the appearance of a complete space, and time also continuously circulates – the past, the present, and the future, all together, connected and in contact. The long-shot aesthetic of the film builds the completeness of the experience. Here Chen Sheng's wounded memories are treated, and self-deliverance is realised. He has seen that even though the young man Weiwei, who represents the future of Chen Sheng's nephew little Weiwei in the symbolic sense, for whom the paths of feeling have not been smooth, is still full of vitality and personality. And having met a woman who looks like his wife, he can at last speak and tell his own story, and face directly his remorse over his mother and wife. The result is that his journey to Zhenyuan is a kind of farewell journey, saying goodbye to his past and restoring his sense of reality. Even though the film has obvious traces of orthodox views, there are many signals that go beyond the requirements of the narrative, the slippery movement of signifiers is anchored in the pursuit of meaning and almost all the form and content are unified.

The wanderings of Chen Sheng have a goal: he intends to search for his lost nephew, and it is precisely this care for his relative that causes him to blunder into this dreamlike place of a simultaneously existing past, present, and future, where he finds comfort for his shattered heart. Meaning and technique, content and form, are effectively integrated in the film to bring out the themes of maintaining values and self-salvation.

In terms of the subject matter, *Kaili Blues* narrates the life and struggles of the underclass, displaying the rough, dilapidated, and poor conditions in Guizhou, and the effects on the countryside of the process of modernisation. The part of Kaili where Chen Sheng lives, a zone where city and countryside come together, makes a sharp contrast to the tall and upright skyscrapers in the distance in Dangmai. The girl the young man Weiwei is in love with, Yangyang, is determined to leave the countryside and go to the city to become a tour guide, while in Zhenyuan Hua Heshang has adopted and is looking after many children whose parents have gone to the city for work and had to leave them behind. Yet this is not a work that can be labelled underclass writing; the predicaments, losses, and gains it presents go beyond the characteristics of the underclass – they could be experienced by anyone. The film uses the artistic technique of long shots and panoramas, creating a space which maintains temporal and spatial continuity and completeness. Space in literature and art is not only physical and psychological; it also must be aesthetic. It is exactly the constructing of this aesthetic space, which has responded to contemporary people's feeling of being adrift, that has broken through the empty illusion of nostalgia's love of the past, and has structured an aesthetic utopia that is a universal complete experience, and in this, people can have a poetic dwelling place.

Looking back over the underclass literature of the present, we can see there is one important problem: when faced with unfeeling reality, many writers persevere with the authenticity of a return to normal life as it was, and have abandoned artistic imagination, filling their works with fictional living just as fragmented as reality. This fills me with regret. The writer Bi Feiyu said, 'It is shameful for a writer to rely too much on imagination,'[16] but in truth, for a writer to rely too much on simply re-presenting reality is also shameful. What is the way out for the underclass? Giving a reply to this problem is perhaps not the main purpose of literature. But as creators of literature and researchers of theory, we must at least give it consideration, and through the aesthetic form of art, provide whatever kind of communal experience we can, create whatever universal meanings we can in order to anchor those fragmented human lives suffering real life misery. As an aspiration for and imagining of a more equitable state of existence and a happier society, the urge for utopia in underclass art is faintly discernible, even pulsating. How to seize this urge, how to construct and display it in a more effective art form, and not allow it to be diffused and scattered in a sentimental nostalgia? This is the problem that underclass literary creation must face up to if it wants to achieve substantial development.

Many people think that underclass art of the new era is a case of good and bad intermingled, with bleak prospects. But the underclass is not a theoretical underclass; it is a real underclass. No matter how much reproach comes from the world of the critics, underclass literature is a product of the times, historically inevitable. Since the 1990s when the problem of the underclass appeared, it has been more than a simple problem of poverty; it is the birth pangs and trauma of China's process of modernisation; it is the sacrifice and price for rapid modernisation. The most obvious difference with the Western underclass is that China's underclass has an exceptionally severe identity anxiety: they are peasants who have lost their land, they are a peasant workforce that is 'unable to enter into the towns and unable to return to the countryside', they are the unemployed of the working class who have lost their identity as workers. The heaviest conflicts of modernity are loaded on their backs, revealing the serious spiritual predicament and value crisis of contemporary society. Writers can and should give them expression in a literary form of profound tragic implications. This is a literary field where there is much to be done. Paying close attention to underclass literature, no matter what the current literary fashion may be, encouraging more penetrating critical responses and more depth of theoretical analysis is, in my view, both necessary and urgent.

NOTES

1. 'New Age' refers to the period of reform and opening up and the socialist building of modernisation since the 1978 third plenum of the 11th Chinese Communist Party Central Committee.
2. Sun Liping, *Fracture: Chinese Society Since the 1990s*, Beijing: Social Science Writings Publishing House, 2003; Sun Liping, *Transformation and Fracture: The Vicissitudes of the Social Structure of Chinese Society since the Reforms*, Beijing: Tsinghua University Press, 2004, Zhuanxing yu duanlie – Gaige Yilai Zhongguo Shehei Jiegou de Bianqian [Transfor-

mation and fracture – the vicissitudes of the social structure of Chinese society since the reforms] (Beijing: Tsinghua University Press, 2004).
3. Jia Yujiao: 'From Institutional Underclass to Systemic Underclass: an Examination of China's Underclass Management Problems based on *The Truly Disadvantaged* by William Julius Wilson', in *Society*, 2009, No.6.
4. Jia Pingwa, 'Gaoxing', *Contemporary*, 2007, No 5.
5. *Ibid.*
6. Chen Yingsong, 'A Dog Called Taiping', *People's Literature*, 2005, No. 10.
7. Li Rui, *Shoulder Pole: The Sixth in the Series of Agricultural Instruments*, Tian Ya, 2010, No 4.
8. Tang Yihong, 'Returning to their old home it's like arriving in a strange land', in *Poets in China*, 2010, No. 4.
9. Henri Lefebvre, 'Space, a Product of Society and its Usefulness', in Bao Yaming, ed., *Modernity and the Production of Space*, p. 48. Shanghai Education Publishing House, 2003.
10. Gaston Pachelard, *The Poetics of Space*, New York: Beacon Press, 1994, p. 137.
11. Chen Yingsong, 'Mother', *Shanghai Literature*, 2016, vol. 10.
12. Jia Pingwa, 'Me and Liu Gaoxing: an epilogue of Gaoxing', in *Mei Wen* (Beautiful Literature), 2007, vol. 8.
13. Chen Yingsong, 'Epilogue' in *Why does the Jaybird Cry*, Wuhan: Yangtze Literature and Arts Publishing House, 2005. p. 408.
14. Wu Min, Xu Li, Huang Huan 'Bi Feiyu: It is shameful for a writer to rely too much on imagination; the present situation is the most difficult to write about', *Southern Daily*, 7 December 2011.
15. Chen Yingsong, *Songya Weishenme Mingjiao – Houji* [Why does the jaybird cry – an epilogue] (Changjian wenyi chubanshe, 2005), 408.
16. Wu Min, Xu Li, Huang Huan, 'Bi Feiyu: Zuojia Guofen Yilai Xiangxiang Kechi Dangdaixing Zuinan Xie' [Bi Feiyu: It is shameful for a writer to rely too much on imagination; the present situation is the most difficult to write about], *Nanfang Ribao*, 7 December 2011.

7
Eco-humanism and the Construction of Eco-aesthetics in China

Xiangzhan Cheng

Eco-aesthetics – or ecological aesthetics – in China began 'officially' in 1994,[1] with Li Xinfu's 'Discussion on Eco-aesthetics'. It has already been developing for twenty-six years and has changed the theoretical structure of China's aesthetics. As summarised by Zeng Fanren:

> In the new age, the establishment of ecological civilisation (i.e., eco-civilisation) has been raised to a greater height than ever before, eco-aesthetics reflects the contemporary aesthetic spirit of the Chinese people's harmonious living together with nature, it is a system for discourse which reflects the tendencies/direction of the values of mainstream society, it is the symbolic aesthetic form for the new age. Eco-aesthetics is coming in from the periphery and entering the mainstream of aesthetics.[2]

This is an accurate assessment of the important position of eco-aesthetics in China, and therefore it is a good entry point for understanding China's contemporary aesthetics.

For the first ten or so years, Chinese eco-aesthetics grew independently, without an understanding of Western eco-aesthetics. Starting from 2009, scholars in China began to introduce Western eco-aesthetics and to research the field in a fully systematic way. Chinese eco-aesthetics, compared with Western eco-aesthetics, generally expresses three distinctive theoretical characteristics. First, it is consciously linked to the resources of China's traditional intellectual culture, thereby realising the transformation of the creativity of China's traditional culture into a force for innovative development'; this appears mainly around the construction of the aesthetics of '*sheng sheng*' 生生 ('creating life').[3] Second, it sees eco-civilisation as the guiding principle in the construction of eco-aesthetics, and as part of its organic composition. Third, it makes eco-humanism its philosophical basis and, in this way, overcomes the anthropocentric tendency of modern aesthetics.

China's eco-aesthetics has already attracted the attention of some international scholars; for example Arnold Berleant from the US and Allen Carlson from Canada have both attempted to introduce it to the academic world of the West, and Chinese scholars have already published some essays in English.[4] But it is necessary to recognise the fact that almost all of the literature on eco-aesthetics in China is written and published in Chinese and therefore has had very little international exposure, and its unique features are not understood by international scholars. This is extremely detrimental to the healthy development of international eco-aesthetics.

Keeping this in mind, this chapter focuses on the third aspect of the above special characteristics of eco-aesthetics in China: the relationship between the construction of Chinese eco-aesthetics and eco-humanism. The first section will introduce Zeng Fanren's eco-aesthetics and its discourse on eco-humanism, which provides the philosophical and theoretical basis for building eco-aesthetics. The second section will introduce the eco-humanist thought of Cheng Xiangzhan's eco-aesthetics, the fundamental core of which is taking an eco-ethical perspective on eco-humanism. The third part considers modern humanism in terms of ecological principles and the practical potential eco-humanism has in regard to the fate of humanity and the life of the planet. Practical value is the direction in which eco-aesthetics is developing.

ECO-HUMANISM AS THE PHILOSOPHICAL BASIS OF ECO-AESTHETICS

Zeng Fanren's *Eco-aesthetics: A Brand New Eco-ontological Aesthetics in the Postmodern Context* (2002) shaped his subsequent discussion. It proposed that eco-aesthetics is a response to the modern context. It is intimately related to the deterioration of the living conditions of humanity – such as environmental degradation, nuclear threat, etc. – and the development of deep ecology. It has played an important role in changing the direction of the aesthetics of the new era and the perspective of literary criticism, and it has promoted both the development of eco-literature and the carrying forward of China's traditional ecological wisdom. Zeng Fanren, in the following years, published five specialist works that develop the theoretical position: *Draft Theory of Eco-ontological Aesthetics* (2003, 2009), *Introduction to Eco-aesthetics* (2010), *Eco-aesthetics in the Dialogue between the West and China* (2012), *Enquiry into, and Dialogue Concerning the Aesthetics of the Era of Eco-civilisation* (2013), and *Research into the Basic Problem of Eco-aesthetics* (2015). These works share a theoretical position embodying the following principles.

First, Zeng Fanren holds that the arrival of the era of eco-civilisation needs to be recognised in the academic world. The changes of the current era include not only economic and social factors but also cultural attitudes. These changes are inevitably seen in literature and art but also in academic disciplines of philosophy and aesthetics. The huge changes in society require that academic research reshape itself to accord with the needs of actual present reality. Eco-aesthetics is just that theoretical reshaping of the academic discipline of aesthetics in the age of eco-civilisation.

Second, ecological, humanist, and aesthetic views must be united. In 2005, Shandong University hosted the 'International Seminar on Aesthetics and Literature from the Perspective of Contemporary Eco-civilisation'. This led to the publication of seminar papers under the title *Man and Nature: Aesthetics and Literature from the Perspective of Contemporary Eco-civilisation*. Zeng Fanren, in his foreword, stated, 'The core problem which needs to be resolved in the establishing of contemporary eco-aesthetics and eco-literature is the combining of the values of ecology, humanism and aesthetics. . . . Contemporary eco-ontological aesthetics is an organic coming together of ecology, humanism, and aesthetics.' Their moving towards unification is necessary to 'realise people's poetic dwelling place'.

Thirdly, Zeng Fanren's eco-aesthetics is different from environmental aesthetics in the West; it is an eco-aesthetics with special Chinese characteristics. Investigation must not only attend to relevant achievements of Western environmental aesthetics, but it must also attend to China's traditional eco-aesthetic wisdom in Confucianism and in such works as the *Book of Changes* (*I Ching* or *Yi Jing*), *Classic of Poetry* (*Shi Jing*), and China's ancient paintings.[5]

Zeng Fanren considers that eco-humanism is 'in fact an integration and reconciliation of anthropocentrism and eco-centrism; it is the new development and extension of humanism for the current era'.[6] This thesis is a reflection of the debate between contemporary anthropocentrism and eco-centrism. The US scholar David Ehrenfeld raised a theoretical proposition in *The Arrogance of Humanism* (1978) about the roots of the theory of the environmental crisis. He considers traditional humanism to be anthropocentric because it concerns itself only with what is beneficial to humankind; it does not concern itself with what benefits nature unless it is intimately connected to human benefit.[7] Scholars have come up with a perspective opposed to humanist anthropocentrism – 'eco-centrism'. The central point of eco-centrism is to emphasise the overall benefit for the eco-sphere and ignore the benefit to the individual, emphasising the absolute equality and inherent value of every type of life. The problem which eco-aesthetics has to face is how to harmonise these opposed outlooks. Zeng Fanren refers to US scholar Aldo Leopold's ecosystems pyramid theory in the 'Land Ethic' (1949) and Rachel Carson's work on food chains, and proposes a new theoretical principle – 'mutual eco-equality' in the food chain. The starting point of our theories is 'improving the happiness of human existence'. This implies that, while we want to take seriously the overall benefit of the ecosystem, we must take even more seriously the future and fate of humankind. To integrate and unify these two approaches is to broaden humanitarianism, extending humankind's spirit of kindliness and love to the entire ecological system: this is eco-humanism. It includes the following key concepts: organic integration, eco-whole, the food chain, the collective, and symbiosis. It is through the integration of these elements that eco-centrism and anthropocentrism can be unified. Zeng Fanren points out that this eco-humanism 'is the philosophical and theoretical foundation for the construction of new eco-aesthetics'.[8]

So, how to construct eco-aesthetics with the new philosophy of eco-humanism as its foundation? Zeng Fenren did not investigate this in detail but proposed another thesis from a different direction: people have a compelling wish to live a beautiful life which comes from their inherent affinity with and love for the natural environment.[9] From this one can construct eco-humanism and one can deduce or construct eco-aesthetics. Eco-humanism and eco-aesthetics are logically joined together. In order to make more prominent the importance of eco-humanism, Zeng Fanren called it 'a new humanist consciousness of the era of eco-civilisation'. But there is still an essential problem which requires further discussion: in the final analysis, what should be the internal logic of the integration of eco-humanism and eco-aesthetics? And, apart from Zeng Fanren's analysis, are there other possibilities? We have our own thoughts and answers to this problem.

ECO-HUMANISM AS THE ESSENTIAL POINT OF ECOLOGICAL AESTHETIC APPRECIATION

My exposition of eco-aesthetics has a latent theoretical framework: the 'aesthetics of *sheng sheng*' which I put forward formally in 2002 (the first '*sheng*' is a verb meaning 'to create'; the second '*sheng*' is a noun meaning 'life'; '*sheng sheng*' thus means to create life so as to make the life process last forever). If we take the traditional Chinese idea of '*sheng sheng*' as the ontology and cultural orientation, and the 'Great Beauty of Heaven and Earth' (*tian di da mei*) as the aesthetic ideal, we have a philosophical framework that can apply to all the aesthetic forms of literature and art. It can apply to ecological concerns as well as to urban environmental matters. It is this '*sheng sheng*' ontology that is the original basis for eco-aesthetics.[10]

We proposed that, beginning from the question of 'values', it can be seen that culture includes both 'civilisation' (*wenming*) and 'anti-civilisation' (*wenbi*). The prerequisite for establishing eco-civilisation is a forceful critique of the numerous and varied malpractices of modern industrial civilisation and its philosophical presuppositions – 'anti-civilisation' – which have created the global environmental crisis and the desertification of people's spiritual world. Modern civilisation is moving toward a recognition that ecological values are the basic principles for creating and preserving civilisation, the only way to avoid the stupid 'drink poison to quench your thirst' suicidal approach of the development route. Therefore, *sheng sheng*-based eco-aesthetics unceasingly criticises the 'nature-killer' tendency of modern industrial civilisation, the 'anti-civilisation'.

Eco-aesthetics, which holds this position, includes four main points. The end-point indicated by this position is 'Ecosophy C', a doctrine which includes eight English technical words beginning with the letter 'C'. The underlying intention is to adopt the key ecological term 'community' (*gongtongti*) as the scientific basis. From the traditional Chinese doctrine of heaven/earth/people, the three influences have been refined to the proposition that 'human life is between heaven and earth'. Holding that heaven, earth, and nature are the parent which gave birth to humanity and its cultural creations, humanity's mission should be to 'assist the natural course of heaven and earth, without daring to act', and 'complement heaven and earth in their transformations and nourishing'. There exists between man, heaven, earth, and the 'myriad things' (*wanwu*) an 'inter-reactional relationship' of penetrating emotional force. This relationship is well suited to being the basis of an aesthetic of appreciation of nature. Therefore, Ecosophy C is a key phrase that connects ancient and modern, East and West, humanities and science, eco-ethics and eco-aesthetics.[11]

We have argued the basic points of ecological aesthetic appreciation and its relation to eco-humanism. The ideological basis of ecological aesthetic appreciation is eco-ethics – the ecological improvement and strengthening of the relationship between the aesthetic and the ethical. Ecological awareness is a necessary pre-condition for ecological aesthetic appreciation.

The 'eco-ethics' or 'ecological awareness' referred to here is in fact 'eco-humanism'. The subject of this chapter's analysis is the fundamental differences between traditional ethics and eco-ethics. The basic difference between the two is their different scope and object: whether or not lifeforms in the biosphere other than humankind can be the subjects of ethics. This is only really asking, 'do life forms apart from humankind possess intrinsic value which is independent of their benefit to humankind?'

The person whose life and writings best represent eco-aesthetics is the famous US ecology scholar Aldo Leopold. He answers the question in the affirmative. His method for establishing the fact of a widening recognition of the sphere of ethical value is the 'concentric circle model': the actual history of ethics in the West has clearly shown the layer-by-layer process of expanding inclusion of subjects in the circle recognised as deserving ethical consideration.[12] The ethical community of ancient Greece consisted of the aristocracy only. Women and slaves were not accepted as part of the ethical community of that time; they were private property, without any human dignity to speak of. That is to say, they were not subjects of ethics. But as history evolved, slave society was eliminated, and women obtained the same level of power as men. In the current era, where the global ecological crisis is worsening day by day, shouldn't humankind continue to broaden the scope of the ethical community, encompassing other living forms apart from humankind? Leopold certainly thinks so. His 'land ethic' theory expanded the definition of community to include all other creatures and the earth itself. It is a foundational work in contemporary eco-ethics and its way of thinking has definite similarities to traditional Confucian ethics. The Confucian doctrine of cultivating one's moral character is in fact really a layer-by-layer expanding 'concentric circle model'. For example, the *Great Learning* (*Da Xue*), in the first section, puts forward 'eight clauses': differentiate things (that is, understand), reach knowledge, have sincere thoughts, rectify your heart, cultivate your self, regulate your family, govern the state, bring peace to all under heaven (that is, the world ruled by the just ruler). This is a layer-by-layer enlarging process – from self to family to state and finally to the whole world. The internal logic of eco-ethics is in fact also a process of a layer-by-layer enlargement: the object of love and care in ethics is the self ('cultivate your self'), this extends to your home ('regulate your family'), and further extends to society ('govern the state'), finally extending to everything in heaven and earth ('bring peace to all under heaven'). On the basis of this model for cultivating your temperament, the philosopher Zhang Zai of the Northern Song Dynasty encapsulated the idea in saying 'the people are my brothers and sisters, [all other] things are my friends'. Wang Yangming of the Ming Dynasty put forward the idea that 'heaven, earth, all the myriad things are a unity'. These can all be seen as rudimentary expressions of eco-ethics. In 'The Change of Direction of Neo-Confucian Humanism', Du Weiming summarises the above ideologies as 'humanism of the Confucian unity of heaven (nature) and man'. He points out that the 'concept of the unity of heaven/nature and man implies that in the context of humankind, there are four inseparable layers: the self, society at large, nature, and heaven above'. Du Weiming in essence sees four aspects: the mutual usefulness between the self and society at large; the sustainable, harmonious relationship between humankind and nature; the mutual motivation of people's hearts and the heavenly way; wisdom (that is, self-knowledge) and self-cultivation – by which the combined virtue or strength of the three powers is achieved.

Synthesising all the old and new, Eastern and Western discourses described above we can see that the core of eco-ethics is nothing more than the layer-by-layer expansion of the 'compassionate heart' from the traditional ethics of the 'person-to-person' relationship to the 'man-to-things' relationship of eco-aesthetics, while at the same time as 'cherishing yourself' and 'cherishing others' also 'cherishing things' – showing love and care for all that lives within the community of life on earth (the ecosphere). One of the symptoms of the environmental crisis is the struggles, even wars, caused by natural-resource scarcity, which is causing the relationship between people to become tense and to deteriorate. The second symptom is 'environmental injustice', which is going from bad to worse, particularly in the disadvantaged sectors of society, which suffer the crisis more acutely. This proves that the environmental crisis has already resulted in a critical deterioration of the traditional 'person-to-person' ethics; 'love for other people' has already become merely exaggerated talk. Considering the way things are, loving 'things' is without doubt an even more rigorous test for human nature. Therefore, advocating the eco-aesthetics of 'loving things' can be seen as both an expectation and a plea for improving disposition and elevating the level of human nature in the age of environmental crisis. Considering that traditional ethical awareness has for a long time included the excellent attribute of 'caring for things', within the meaning of eco-ethics 'loving things' is certainly not impossible. The crux is whether or not there is an expansive 'compassionate heart'; and this sense of 'compassionate heart' is the ecological solicitude of the era of ecological crisis.

We summarise this eco-ethics as 'humanism with an emphasis on the whole of the ecosphere' – abbreviated to 'eco-humanism'. It includes two main points. The first is 'the whole ecosphere', which makes explicit that the 'whole' is neither the entire solar system nor the entire universe, but the only life-supporting ecosphere so far discovered, the earth. This is the specific 'whole'. The intention of defining the 'whole' in this way does not imply that we have overlooked the ultimate or metaphysical meanings within 'ecological care'; in the course of our experiencing ecological aesthetic appreciation, we can without doubt include the 'big picture' significance of 'universal consciousness' and 'universal experiencing'. Nonetheless, the 'whole' referred to here is the entire ecosphere of the earth. The reasons for this limitation are twofold: the whole universe is far beyond the current knowledge of humankind, and 'humanism', at the same time as opposing 'anthropocentrism', also emphasises 'putting people first'. The doctrine of eco-humanism has as its final goal the long-term, high-quality existence of humankind (it is not for the sake of the propagation of ants, flies, or any other type of thing). Humankind not only sets the parameters for the entire ecosphere, but its quality of life is also the final frame of reference for judging whether or not the ecological conditions of this entirety are in a state of equilibrium (the final frame of reference is not giant pandas or sweet potatoes). The ethical attitude of 'loving things' included within eco-humanism can be called eco-consciousness; it is the basis of ecological aesthetic appreciation.

Eco-aesthetics and traditional aesthetics have obvious differences; the four most important points can be summarised as 'one prerequisite, three procedures'. The 'one prerequisite' refers to aesthetic engagement replacing the verb–object 'appreciating beauty'. The reason for this is to clarify the persistent mistake of the dominant aesthetic appreciation theory – assuming antagonistic dualism between subject and object. The three procedures have a step-by-step progress and layer-by-layer deepening relationship. First, there is ecological consciousness and traditional aesthetic appreciation, which are the bases for the turn towards eco-aesthetics. With gaining ecological knowledge, eco-aesthetics will intensify and there will be unequivocal understanding of the predilections of human aesthetics and the disaster they have created; finally, there will be conscious self-examination and introspection, and critique of traditional aesthetic appreciation to attain ecological aesthetic appreciation.[13] It is exactly through this kind of analysis that we examine the basic intentions of eco-humanism, and its connection with eco-aesthetics.

ECO-AESTHETICS' CRITICISM OF THE PRACTICAL AESTHETICS OF LI ZEHOU

With regards to the actual context of contemporary aesthetics in China, our 'eco-aesthetic' conception is by no means random; it has a clear target to focus on, and criticise – Li Zehou's practical aesthetics, which occupies the dominant position in China. Li Zehou has continuously emphasised people. For example, when analysing the philosophical basis of his aesthetics, 'anthropological ontology philosophy' or 'the practical philosophy of subjectivity', he clearly sets out that 'the fundamental philosophical proposition of anthropological ontology is the destiny of humans'. Hence, in his view the first question has become 'what possibilities are there for humankind?'[14] This, in the special environment of the liberated thinking in China in the 1980s, had a huge influence, and greatly promoted the broad transmission and recognition of Li Zehou's aesthetics.

However, the 'people' philosophy of Li Zehou at that time, as he himself has said, 'had its origins in philosophy since Kant'; and 'people', in the modern subjective philosophical sense, is also the 'people' of modern humanism. People in this sense is the subject in modern Western philosophy, and the world which corresponds to this is awaiting humankind's understanding; even as it conquers the 'object', the relationship between people and world has indeed formed into such a subject–object opposition of understanding and conquest. Therefore, this 'person' can be summarised as a 'subject' – the knower and subjugator – situated in opposition to the objective world. Li Zehou's *Four Lectures on Aesthetics* quotes the following passage from his own *Critique of Critical Philosophy*; this is sufficient to show how seriously he takes it:

> Through a lengthy history of societal practice, nature has been humanised, human purpose has been objectified. Nature has been controlled and remoulded by humankind, conquered, and put to use, it has become nature that obeys humans, has become humans' 'inorganic vehicle', humans have become the master who has control over nature.[15]

This is a strong declaration about how humankind has used nature and then conquered nature; it is also the most clamorous sound of Li Zehou's people philosophy and the practical aesthetics that he evolved. Within such theses, humans have had the temerity to become the 'master of nature'; and the foundation of the so-called 'essence of beauty' is inevitably the 'humanisation of nature'. Li Zehou's aesthetics in this way carried with it an extremely strong anthropocentric colour. This aesthetics naturally became the supreme object of criticism for Chinese eco-aesthetics.

I have previously drawn on Gibson's ecological-psychology theories to interpret the essentials of eco-aesthetics, and to criticise Li Zehou's aesthetics. Gibson holds that the natural environment has provided animals with numerous means for survival, and different animals have different ways of surviving: 'specific habitats will imply a certain animal, and this type of animal implies a certain habitat'.[16] If animals are taken from their original habitat then they are no longer the same animal. Humankind often builds zoos for visitors to appreciate animals, building replicas of their habitats, but we must be fully aware that these animals are already a very long way from their original habitat, and their natural instincts, which are inextricably linked to their living environment, which has already been all but lost. Humankind can no doubt 'appreciate' the beauty of these animals, and appreciate them as aesthetic objects, but this is already worlds apart from the ecological aesthetic appreciation that we are analysing here – that is, the objects of ecological aesthetic appreciation are animals living in their original habitats. What is appreciated is, as Gibson says, '*how* the animals live, not *where* they live'. Only in relation to their original habitat can the natural instincts of animals be manifested in the most natural and complete way. The habitat which is most closely related to the animals quite naturally becomes the rich source for direct aesthetic experience. For example, when we appreciate the beauty of the red-crowned crane in the unspoiled wilderness, the 'marshland' which is the habitat of the red-crowned crane will also be appreciated by us at the same time because (based on fundamental ecological knowledge) we would know that if there were no marshland there would be no red-crowned cranes. The beauty of red-crowned cranes can very easily become the object of peoples' appreciation, but amongst those 'appreciators' who are well educated in ecology, quite ordinary marshland, a blade of grass, a puddle, a lump of mud, a leech, etc., are all appreciated because they make up part of an organically formed bio-community and an ecological system. These objects are not 'beautiful' things in the traditional sense – they are even 'ugly' – however, this absolutely does not prevent them from becoming fascinating 'objects of aesthetic appreciation'. Those appreciators with a high level of ecological education can learn from this about the natural world's mysterious creative strength. This kind of aesthetics is most in keeping with the classic definition of ecology: organisms and their interaction with the environment. The key reason Gibson calls his theory of observational awareness 'an ecological approach' is that he is more thorough than most ecologists, elaborating in greater depth the inherent relationship between animals and their habitat.

The difference between the modern aesthetics represented by Li Zehou's practical aesthetics in China and the essentials of eco-aesthetics can be summarised in three points: (1) Respect for the natural conditions of things themselves and not seeing them in human terms. This is a world apart from recognising the 'source of beauty' as being in the 'humanisation of nature'. (2) Fundamental ecological knowledge plays a very significant role in eco-aesthetics; it inspires and guides the imagination and feelings of appreciators. (3) The traditional idea of 'beauty' can in no way describe ecologically aware aesthetic activity and the objects of its appreciation. The word 'beauty' should be superseded by the key terms 'aesthetic object' and its 'positive aesthetic value'. Li Zehou's aesthetic framework, because it has confused 'beauty' and 'aesthetic object', cannot explain the wider vision of eco-aesthetics, and so gives rise to misguided concepts like 'ecological beauty'.[17] In opposition to Li Zehou's 'practical aesthetics' and the 'humanisation of nature', we put forward as the core proposition for eco-aesthetics the 'naturalisation of nature' (i.e., treating the natural world as, in fact, natural). In China, 'practical aesthetics', with Li Zehou as its representative, explains the appreciation of beauty through the 'humanisation of nature', now so well-known it has become an entry in the *Encyclopedia of Aesthetics* (of which Li Zehou was one of the main editors!):

> Through a lengthy history of societal production practice, humankind has fundamentally transformed its relationship with nature, nature has been controlled, subjugated, transformed, and utilised, the aims of humans have been realised within nature.[18]

From the position of eco-humanism, 'the humanisation of nature' is an inadequate proposition. It emphasises only the 'humanisation' of nature, but it neglects three important related problems: For what reason is it humanised? How is it humanised? What are the limits of humanisation? From the ecological point of view, responses to these problems are as follows: (1) To create ecological civilisation. (2) At the philosophical level, what the principle of humanising stresses: 'assisting the transforming and nourishing powers of heaven and earth',[19] which mainly applies to the natural world which has not yet been transformed by humankind. At the level of science and technology, it lays stress on obeying the principles of restoration ecology,[20] which applies mainly to the parts of nature which have already been ruined by humankind. (3) The limitation of humanisation is the extent to which nature can support it.[21] Therefore, in the era of eco-civilisation, we must, from the point of view of ecological values, reflect on and criticise the traditional proposition of the 'humanisation of nature', advocating from the point of view of eco-ethics and restoration ecology its opposite, the 'naturalisation of nature'. And we must uphold 'respect for nature, conform to nature, conserve nature', as stated in the report of the Eighteenth National Congress of the CCP: humankind, as the subject of the creation of civilisation, as ethical in conduct, must respect nature. In its modes of production and lifestyle it must conform to nature, and in its mode of behaviour it must preserve nature.

'The aesthetic' is at the core of aesthetics theory; therefore 'ecological aesthetic appreciation' is the core and object of study of eco-aesthetics. So far, as far the ideological theme is concerned, eco-aesthetics is an aesthetic reflection on the cultural evils of humankind;[22] it indeed enriches this theoretical proposition of 'naturalisation of nature'. It is precisely because large-scale cultural malpractice exists and worsens day by day that we from the heights of eco-values advocate the aesthetic proposition 'all virgin nature is good aesthetically' – the nature which has not been transformed or polluted by humankind, existing in its original state, for example unadulterated 'blue sky, green land, clear water'. Eco-aesthetics is concerned that all have an affirmative aesthetic value; they are all 'beautiful' and 'good' – because these natural things are the purest, and have most thoroughly broken free of the 'humanisation' created by humankind's 'uncivilised behaviour', their cultural malpractice.

China's contemporary natural aesthetics is based on the concept of the 'humanisation of nature'; thinking of natural things that 'their beauty is not intrinsic, but is only made known through man'.[23] Our eco-aesthetics is completely different from this; we believe natural things are beautiful and good aesthetically in themselves: 'beautiful things have their own beauty/beauty is beautiful of itself'. Humans are the appreciators of natural things, not their transformer (even less are they their owner, or plunderer). The usefulness of eco-aesthetics is mainly in displaying the fascinating charm that nature had in the first place, making natural things appear in the state which they themselves naturally have – 'manifesting through humans'. The aesthetics of the era of eco-civilization must inevitably be eco-aesthetics, aesthetics which has as its ontology the universal '*sheng sheng*' force, an aesthetics which has 'the virtuous power of *sheng sheng*' as its values; it is in fact an 'aesthetics of *sheng sheng*'.[24] Only in this way can human civilization avoid obliteration and attain continuous regeneration. The building of a 'beautiful China'[25] advocated by our nation has clear aesthetic targets – blue sky, green land, clear water. This is exactly the direction in which eco-aesthetics must exert itself. Simply put, the essence of the theory of eco-aesthetics, advocating the proposition of 'naturalisation of nature' (the '*sheng sheng* aesthetics' we are advocating) can be summarised in these four expressions: the beautiful is beautiful in itself, by itself and for itself; it is displayed through people; what eco-aesthetics promotes is ecological aesthetic appreciation; and only with this can we regenerate without ceasing.[26]

CONCLUSION

The famous Tang Dynasty poet Bai Juyi said 'memorials are written for the times, poems are written about actual things'. The construction of eco-aesthetics is not learned writings in an ivory tower, but is something 'for the times' and 'about actual things'. The 'times' are now, the era of eco-crisis; the 'actual thing' is rescue from environmental crisis. Eco-humanism has made clear that the main cause of the global environmental crisis is human activity. We must exert ourselves conscientiously to take on the great responsibility that humankind bears for the good health of the ecosystem. Eco-aesthetics based on this value approach reflects anew on the aesthetic activities and the practical experience of humankind. Drawing lessons from the basic principles of ecology, we can facilitate the ecological reshaping of aesthetics and making it an organic component of eco-civilisation.

Li Zehou once judged eco-aesthetics as 'aesthetics without people', which is really the greatest misunderstanding of eco-aesthetics. Of course, eco-aesthetics puts great importance on people, but not the type of person in Li Zehou's aesthetics – people who see themselves as 'masters of nature' – but those 'ecological people' who exist within the ecosystem, who have an ecological self. Simply put, eco-aesthetics exerts itself to make more conspicuous people's eco-dimensionality; it is a new type of aesthetics which combines ecological, humanist, and aesthetic values: at its core it uses ecology to reshape modern humanist and aesthetic values.[27] Finally, the purpose of constructing eco-aesthetics is not simply to guide humankind in extricating itself from the ecological crisis and surviving. More important, through fulfilling our own ecological responsibilities, consciousness is raised and character developed – it becomes more meaningful to be alive. The development of eco-aesthetics is based on reflections on the positive qualities and demerits of modern humanist theory, enriching eco-humanism, investigating its relation to eco-aesthetics, and making eco-aesthetics a responsible, caring aesthetics, concerned both with the fate of humankind and with the community of life on earth.

NOTES

1. Li Xinfu, 'Lun Shengtai Meixue' [Discussion on ecoaesthetics], *Nanjing Shehui Kexue* 12 (1994).
2. Zeng Fanren, 'Fazhan Shengtai Meixue, Jianshe Meili Zhongguo' [Developing ecoaesthetics, building up a beautiful China], *Renmin Ribao*, 22 June 2018.
3. Cheng Xiangzhan, *Sheng Sheng Meixue Luntai – Cong Wenyi Meixue dao Shengtai Meixue* [Collected writings on aesthetics of *sheng sheng*: From literary and arts aesthetics to eco-aesthetics] (Beijing: Renmin chubanshe, 2012).
4. See Cheng Xiangzhan, 'Ecosophy and Ecoaesthetics: A Chinese Perspective', in Hubert Zapf, ed., *Handbook of Ecocriticism and Cultural Ecology* (Berlin: De Gruyter, 2016), 481-493; Cheng Xiangzhan, 'Some Critical Reflections on Berleantian Critique of Kantian Aesthetics from the Perspective of Eco-aesthetics', *Espes* 6 (2) (December 2017): 30–39.
5. Zeng Fanren, preface to *Ren yu Ziran: Dangdai Shengtai Wenming Shiye Zhong de Meixue yu Wenxue*, Zeng Fanren, ed. [People and nature: On aesthetics and literature within the field of contemporary eco-civilisation] (Zhengzhou: Henan renmin chubanshe, 2006), 2, 3.
6. Zeng Fanren, *Shengtai Meixue Daolun* [Introduction to eco-aesthetics] (Beijing: Shangwu yinshuguan, 2010), 64.
7. Daiwei Ailunfeierde [David Ehrenfeld], *Rendaozhuyi de Jianwang* [The arrogance of humanism], trans. Li Yunlong (Beijing: Guoji wenhua chubanshe, 1988). Originally published in English by Oxford University Press (1981). Here we have directly translated 'humanitarianism' and 'humanism'.
8. Zeng Fanren, *Shengtai Meixue Daolun*, 64.
9. Zeng Fanren, *Shengtai Meixue Daolun*, 64.
10. Cheng Xiangzhan, 'Zhongguo Zhouxinqi de "Sheng Sheng" Guannian yu Dangdai Shengtai Meixue Jiangou' [The conception of '*sheng sheng*' in China's axial period and the construction of a contemporary eco-aesthetics], in Zeng Fanren, ed., *Ren yu Ziran: Dangdai Shengtai Wenming Shiye Zhong de Meixue yu Wenxue*.
11. Cheng Xiangzhan, 'Ecosophy and Ecoaesthetics'.

12. Sociologist Ernest Burgess first proposed the concentric circle theory in 1925. His theory was among the first to explain urban social structure and its evolution. See Hans Blumenfeld, 'On the Concentric-Circle Theory of Urban Growth', *Land Economics* 25 (2) (May 1949): 209–212.
13. Cheng Xiangzhan, 'On the Four Keystones of Ecological Aesthetic Appreciation', in Simon C. Estok and Won-Chung Kim, eds., *East Asian Ecocriticisms: A Critical Reader* (New York: Palgrave Macmillan, 2013), 213–228.
14. Li Zehou, *Hua Xie Meixue: Meixue Si Jiang* [Hua Xia aesthetics: Four lectures on aesthetics] (Beijing: Sanlian shudian, 2008), 263.
15. Li Zehou, *Hua Xie Meixue*, 281.
16. James Gibson, *The Ecological Approach to Visual Perception* (New Jersey: Lawrence Erlbaum Associates, 1986), 128.
17. Cheng Xiangzhan, 'Lun Shengtai Meixue de Meixueguan yu Yanjiu Duixiang – Jianlun Li Zehou Meixue Moshi de Quexian' [Discussions on the aesthetic viewpoint and objects of research of eco-aesthetics – also on the shortcomings of Li Zehou's aesthetic view and aesthetic model], *Tianjin Shehui Kexue* 1 (2015): 136–142.
18. Li Zehou and Ru Xin, eds., *Meixue Baike Quanshu* [Encyclopedia of aesthetics] (Beijing: Shehui kexue wenxian chubanshe, 1990), 714.
19. The *Zhong Yong* (Doctrine of the Mean) says: 'It is only he who is possessed of the most complete sincerity that can exist under heaven, who can give its full development to his nature. Able to give its full development to his own nature, he can do the same to the nature of other men. Able to give its full development to the nature of other men, he can give their full development to the natures of animals and things. Able to give their full development to the natures of creatures and things, he can assist the transforming and nourishing powers of heaven and earth. Able to assist the transforming and nourishing powers of heaven and earth, he may with heaven and earth form a ternion' (*Wei tianxia zhicheng, wei neng jinqixing; neng jinqixing, ze neng jin renzhi xing;neng jin renzhixing, ze neng jin wuzhixing;neng jin wuzhixing, ze keyi zan tiandi zhi huayu; keyi zan tiandi zhi huayu, ze keyi yu tiandi can ye*).
20. Restoration Ecology is the science of the research into the reason for the degeneration of ecosystems, the technology and methods for recovering and rebuilding degenerated ecosystems, and the processes and mechanisms of ecology. Generally, there are not many objections to this definition, but regarding what it includes and how far it extends, there are many different understandings and have been many investigations. The 'restoration' referred to here indicates the reproducing

of an ecosystem's original appearance or original function; 'rebuilding', however, indicates, in a situation where it is impossible or unnecessary to reproduce the original ecosystem, constructing an ecosystem that is not an exact duplicate of the past, or is even completely new. Restoration has already been used as a generalised technical term, including the meanings of rebuilding, refurbishing, transforming, replanting, normally giving a general sense of improving and rebuilding degenerated ecosystems, making them suitable for re-use, restoring their biological potential, this can be called ecological restoration.

21. The normal word we use is the English 'sustainability', the meaning of the root word 'sustain' is to preserve, support, endure, etc., therefore, this word can also be translated as 'affordability' (*kechengshouxing*); this clearly shows that the ability of ecosystems to support human culture is absolutely not unlimited. Another way of putting it, the ability of nature to support it, has decided (the word used is regulate) the limits of the development of human culture – human culture cannot develop immoderately and unlimitedly.
22. '*Wenbi*' 文弊is a technical term previously formulated by the author. Its meaning encapsulates 'cultural evils', that is, the negative side of 'humanisation' and its negative consequences. See Cheng Xiangzhan, 'Cong "Wenbi" Gainian Kan "Shengtai Wenming" de Lilun Neihan' [Looking at the theoretical implications of 'eco-civilization' from the perspective of '*wenbi*'], *Nanjing Linye Daxue Xuebao* 2 (2015): 53–58.
23. The Tang Dynasty intellectual Liu Zongyuan, in his essay 'A Diary of Yongzhou Matui Mountain Thatched Hut', wrote: 'Now a beauty spot is only made manifest when men praise it [*mei bu zi mei, yin ren er zhang*; a non-poetic translation would be 'beauty is not beautiful of itself; it becomes manifest because of humans'], if the Orchid Pavilion had not met with You Jun, its clear brook and luxuriant bamboo would have become overgrown in the empty hills.' Ye Lang gave this the highest praise, stating that these eight characters 'are greater than an entire book', being a 'proposition of extreme importance which touches upon the essence of aesthetic activity'. Ye Lang, Xiong Zhong zhi Zhu – Zouxiang Xiandai zhi Zhongguo Meixue [The bamboo in our hearts, moving towards the modern Chinese aesthetic] (Hefei: Anhui jiaoyu chubanshe, 1998), 84, 101.
24. Cheng Xiangzhan, *Sheng Sheng Meixue Luntai*. *Sheng sheng* is a concept that can be understood as borrowing the ancient Chinese proposition of '*li yi fen shu*' 理一分殊 ('the overall pattern is a unity, but its manifestations are many'; its origins are in Song Dynasty neo-Confucianism,

albeit with roots in ancient thought). This concept can be an ontology, a value system, and has been put to use in many different aesthetic fields, for example art aesthetics, environmental aesthetics, somaesthetics, the aesthetics of daily life. The author's research in aesthetics is built on the concept of '*sheng sheng*', therefore it can be called an 'aesthetics of *sheng sheng*'.

25. 'Beautiful China' was a new standpoint put forward as one of the keywords for guiding China's future development in the report of the Eighteenth National Congress of the Chinese Communist Party, 9 November 2012.
26. Cheng Xiangzhan, 'Wumai Tianqi de Shengtai Meixue Sikao – Jianlun "Ziran de Ziranhua" Mingti yu Sheng Sheng Meixue de Yaoyi' [Meditations on smoggy weather from the perspective of eco-aesthetics – also on the 'nature naturalising' proposition and the essential meaning of aesthetics of *sheng sheng*], *Zhongzhou Xuekan* 1 (2015): 153–168.
27. Concerning Li Zehou's refutation, see Cheng Xiangzhan, 'Zhongguo Shengtai Meixue de Chuangxinxing Jiangou Guocheng Jiqi Shengtai Renwenzhuyi Sixiang Lichang – Jingda Li Zehou Xiansheng' [The process of creative construction of Chinese eco-aesthetics and its eco-humanist thinking standpoint – a respectful response to Mr Li Zehou], *Dongnan Xueshu* 1 (2020).

Notes on Contributors

CAO, QING is Associate Professor in Chinese studies in the School of Modern Languages and Cultures, Durham University. His research centres on the mass media and social changes in modern China. He is the author of *China under Western Gaze: Representing China in the British Television Documentaries, 1980–2000* (2014). His most recent publications include a co-edited book, *Brand China in the Media: Transformation of Identities* (2019).

CHENG, XIANGZHAN is Distinguished Changjiang Professor of aesthetics, Deputy Dean of the School of Literature at Shandong University, China, Deputy Director of Shandong University Research Center for Ecological Civilization and Ecoaesthetics, a visiting scholar of the Harvard-Yenching Institute at Harvard University (2006–2007), the executive editor of *Newsletter on Eco-aesthetics and Eco-criticism*, and a member of the international advisory board of *Contemporary Aesthetics*. His fields of research include the history of Chinese aesthetics, environmental aesthetics, ecological aesthetics (i.e., eco-aesthetics). His most recent books are *A Study of Environmental Assessment and Planning* (2013) and *An Introduction to Eco-aesthetics* (2020). Eight of his publications on ecological aesthetics are cited in the 'Environmental Aesthetics' page of the *Stanford Encyclopedia of Philosophy* (Summer 2019 edition).

COLLINS, CHARLES graduated in Chinese (first class) from School of Oriental and African Studies (SOAS), University of London, in 1982. Immediately, he moved to China and, up until his recent decision to return to study, has held a variety of management positions in the business world: a pioneering Japanese/Swiss container shipping agency in Beijing; an international trading and investment company in Shanghai, and back to the UK in 2002 as China Sales Director for a Luton-based engineering company. In 2017, wanting to fulfil his ambition to know the great works of Chinese literature, he went back to SOAS to follow their Sinology MA course.

MANOR-PERCIVAL, YONIT is a former journalist and now an academic and a lawyer currently practicing with a Chinese law firm. Dr Manor-Percival studied and worked in the People's Republic of China (PRC) and advised Chinese corporations in relation to their overseas operations for many years. As an academic she specialises and lectures on the interface between law, society, and corporations within the framework of the global political economy with a focus on the PRC.

MARGOLIES, DAVID is Emeritus Professor of English, Goldsmiths, University of London. He has published extensively on Shakespeare and on Marxist literary criticism. He was editor of *Red Letters: A Journal of Cultural Politics* and the journal *Green Socialist.* His particular concern is culture's potential as a political force. His most recent book is *Culture and Politics: Selected Writings of Christopher Caudwell* (2018).

WANG, JIE is Distinguished Changjiang Professor and Deputy Dean of the Faculty of Arts and Humanities, and Director of the Centre for Contemporary Marxist Aesthetics at the College of Media and International Culture, Zhejiang University. He currently serves as Vice-President of the Chinese Association of Aesthetics and Vice-President of Chinese Association of Anthropology of Arts. He is editor-in-chief of the journal *Research on Marxist Aesthetics.* As principal investigator, he has been leading a major national research project *Fundamental Questions of Contemporary Aesthetics and Criticism.* His major monographs include *Looking for Utopia: Crises and Reconstruction of Modern Aesthetics, Culture and Society: Marxism and the Development of Chinese Literature Theory in the 20th Century.* His major translated books include *Culture, Governance and Society* and *Aesthetic Idealism.* His major edited books include *Aesthetics.*

XU, JIAONA obtained her PhD from Nanjing University and is currently Associate Professor in the School of Literature and Journalism,

Hanshan Normal University. Her main areas of research include modern literary theory and Marxist aesthetics. She is currently completing a book entitled *The Theory of Aesthetic Ideology in Western Marxism* which is sponsored by the Social Science Foundation of the Chinese National Department of Education. She is co-translator of *Critical Theory and the Crisis of Contemporary Capitalism* by Heiko Feldner and Fabio Vighi (the Chinese version published by Oriental Publishing Center, 2020).

YIN, QINGHONG obtained his PhD in the Department of Chinese Language and Literature in Nanjing University. He is a lecturer in the Faculty of Humanities in Shanghai Jiao Tong University and he is also the Director of the Research Center on Aesthetics, Art and Culture Theory. His research interests are critical theory, cultural identity, and anthropology of art.

YANG, ZHOU obtained her PhD in modern languages and cultures from Durham University. Her academic focus on the construction of cultural modernity amongst Chinese intelligentsia from the early twentieth century. Yang's research is particularly interested in the utopian notion present in the interplay between translation and creative writing in China under the influence of English romanticism and French symbolist poetry. Her recent publications include a chapter 'Chineseness in Bian Zhilin's pre-war poetry' in *China's Contemporary Image and Rhetoric Practice* (2021).

Index

Thanks to our Patreon subscriber:

Ciaran Kane

Who has shown generosity and comradeship in support of our publishing.